New Readings

George Eliot

KU-545-283

HARVESTER
New Readings

George Eliot

Simon Dentith

Lecturer in English
Liverpool University

THE HARVESTER PRESS

First published in Great Britain in 1986 by
THE HARVESTER PRESS LIMITED
Publisher: John Spiers
16 Ship Street, Brighton, Sussex

British Library Cataloguing in Publication Data

Dentith, Simon
  George Eliot. — (Harvester new readings
  series)
  1. Eliot, George — Criticism and
  interpretation
  I. Title
  823'.8   PR4688

  ISBN 0-7108-0588-8
  ISBN 0-7108-0598-5 Pbk

Typeset in 11/13pt Goudy by Witwell Ltd

Printed in Great Britain by
Mackays of Chatham Ltd., Kent

THE HARVESTER PRESS PUBLISHING GROUP
The Harvester Press Group comprises Harvester Press Ltd (chiefly
publishing literature, fiction, philosophy, psychology, and science
and trade books); Harvester Press Microform Publications Ltd
(publishing in microform unpublished archives, scarce printed
sources, and indexes to these collections) and Wheatsheaf Books
Ltd (chiefly publishing in economics, international politics,
sociology, women's studies and related social sciences); Certain
Records Ltd and John Spiers Music Ltd (music publishing).

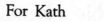

For Kath

Harvester New Readings

This major new paperback series offers a range of important new critical introductions to English writers, responsive to new bearings which have recently emerged in literary analysis. Its aim is to make more widely current and available the perspectives of contemporary literary theory, by applying these to a selection of the most widely read and studied English authors.

The range of issues covered varies with each author under survey. The series as a whole resists the adoption of general theoretical principles, in favour of the candid and original application of the critical and theoretical models found most appropriate to the survey of each individual author. The series resists the representation of any single either traditionally or radically dominant discourse, working rather with the complex of issues which emerge from a close and widely informed reading of the author in question in his or her social, political and historical context.

The perspectives offered by these lucid and accessible introductory books should be invaluable to students seeking an understanding of the full range and complexity of the concerns of key canonical writers. The major concerns of each author are critically examined and sympathetically and lucidly reassessed, providing indispensable handbooks to the work of major English authors seen from new perspectives.

David Aers	*Chaucer*
Drummond Bone	*Byron*
Angus Calder	*T.S. Eliot*
Simon Dentith	*George Eliot*
Kelvin Everest	*Keats*
Kate Flint	*Dickens*
Paul Hamilton	*Wordsworth*
Brean Hammond	*Pope*
Kiernan Ryan	*Shakespeare*
Simon Shepherd	*Spenser*
Nigel Wood	*Swift*

Contents

Acknowledgements

I would like to thank a number of people who have helped in the writing of this book. Kelvin Everest, Susie Meikle, Katharine Dentith and Philip Dodd all read the manuscript at various stages of preparation, and I have gratefully incorporated many of their suggestions. Bill Myers kindly let me read a copy of his book, *The Teaching of George Eliot*, prior to publication. I have also benefited from reading some unpublished work by Rick Rylance on the social history of Coventry and its use in *Middlemarch*. Finally I am especially grateful to Olivia Gould for her skill with the typewriter.

Introduction

George Eliot's novels—there are only eight of them, if you count *Scenes of Clerical Life* as just one novel—have today a considerable presence in our cultural and educational institutions. Over a hundred years after George Eliot's death in 1880, they are widely published in paperback, and figure prominently in bookshops—or at least in some bookshops. They appear centrally on school, college and university syllabuses, and bear the weight of long discussions, essays and exam answers: indeed, you are probably reading this book as part of your work in an educational institution of some kind. They are the subject of scholarly books and articles, and occasionally appear as adaptations on the television. As the occasion for all this discussion and debate and interpretation, the novels have come to carry a wide variety of messages and meanings, some even mutually contradictory; messages and meanings addressed to the way we live now, both privately and publicly, and to the ways we understand society and historical change.

The novels have not always occupied so central a place,

however, either in the syllabuses of 'English' or in critical understanding of the history of the English novel. The story of George Eliot's reputation is itself highly suggestive of shifts and alterations in taste and understanding over the last hundred years, and through them of transformations in the relations between culture and society. Capable in her own lifetime, as we shall see, of appealing to very different audiences, both of intellectuals like herself and of the ordinary middle-class patrons of the circulating libraries from where her books were borrowed, she was valued both as a wise teacher and as an approachable story-teller. After her death, however, though her novels never failed to attract a readership, her reputation suffered with the revaluation of all things 'Victorian' which began at least twenty years before the death of the Queen. Her novels were felt to offend against canons of art now often understood in an aesthetic or 'art for art's sake' way; self-consciously and explicitly didactic, they represented precisely what critics of the 1880s and 1890s felt to be most oppressive about high Victorian notions of art. Where they were defended, such as by the great nineteenth-century man of letters Leslie Stephen, it was above all the early novels—*Adam Bede*, *Mill on the Floss* and *Silas Marner*—that were felt to be most admirable; they represented, he claimed, the peculiar charm of unforced descriptions of an English country life now fast vanishing. His daughter, Virginia Woolf, praised the novels in a review in 1919, effecting the important revaluation of *Middlemarch* with the famous remark that it was 'one of the few English novels written for grown-up people';[1] but it was above all F.R. Leavis, in some celebrated articles in *Scrutiny* and then in *The Great Tradition* (1947), who claimed the importance for George Eliot which is now used to justify her central position in English studies. For Leavis and the *Scrutiny* group, engaged in their own battle against what they saw as cultural dilettantism on the one hand and a mechanical and commercialised civilisation on the other, Eliot's novels, especially *Middlemarch*, could be used to assert the possibility and indeed the necessity of a serious and mature art which was both poised and moral—not in the Victorian didactic sense, but moral in the capacity to render the important human decisions in all the specificity and with all the nuances of real human lives.

Leavis's views, on this and other matters, were the dominant ones in English studies (in Britain at least) in the 1950s and 1960s; indeed, they were remarkably influential in English culture more generally. Since the 1960s, however, his views, and those other more traditional positions which I have briefly sketched in, have come under increasing fire. This has not simply been because of a natural evolution of ideas. The current situation in English studies, characterised by intense debate and controversy, reflects a wider crisis in social and cultural life, which has thrown up a number of radical (and sometimes not so radical) intellectual positions challenging the apparently commonsense presuppositions not only in literary studies, but also in sociology, philosophy, anthropology and many other subjects. I shall name just three of the main contenders in a very complex situation. There has been a resurgence of Marxism, not only as a political stance but as a mode of intellectual inquiry. From quite another direction, structuralism at one time seemed to promise a rigorous account of many cultural phenomena, including literature, in terms which stressed how such phenomena had their own systematic and autonomous logics. More recently, deconstruction, taking its inspiration from the work of the French philosopher Derrida, has had considerable impact on literary studies especially in America. The procedures of deconstruction are various, but it does characteristically seek to undermine the apparently secure foundations of philosophical or literary statements.

How has George Eliot fared amid this flurry of competing

3

positions? What requires emphasis is that none of these positions is without implications in social or even political terms. This is obviously the case with Marxism, but structuralism and deconstruction also bear traces, in different ways, of the social and political crises which spawned them, and which lend them their current urgency. Structuralism, in one of its guises, seems to offer a scientific and value-free description of cultural phenomena, and deconstruction, in America at least, offers the appearance of radicalism to an academic avant-garde. So George Eliot's writings, with their own weight of social (and even political) meanings, cannot simply be assimilated to give a structuralist reading, a Marxist reading, a deconstructive reading, and so on. It should be said, however, that given the professional and political insulation of the academic profession, there have been some attempts along those lines. Nevertheless, in general terms George Eliot is committed both to realism and to a notion of personal selfhood; these are exactly the ideas that have been the subject of severe and sometimes acute criticism by both structuralism and deconstruction. Indeed, to the extent that one version of an academic Marxism has been affected by these currents of thought, here too George Eliot's realism has seemed suspect—though Marxists have ample enough ground for being wary of George Eliot anyway. Overall, then, George Eliot's novels have proved an unattractive topic for critics of these persuasions. Indeed, we can put it more strongly. In so far as these positions habitually promote writing which is, in their own terms, 'open' or 'productive' or 'readerly', they tend to rely on contrasts with writing which is 'closed' 'realist' or 'writerly'. George Eliot has been a principal sufferer in this process, serving as an Aunt Sally by which to measure the excellences of modernist writing.[2]

The following book is, in the broadest terms, a defence of George Eliot as a realist writer. In the present cultural situation, it seems to me to be essential to hold on to a belief that society and social change are susceptible to rational and secular understanding. In her own terms, George Eliot offers the most sustained and ambitious attempt at providing such an understanding in English literature. I have, naturally, tried to assimilate some elements of the critique of realism as it has been made in English studies. However, the book that follows is in no way a *review* of structuralist, deconstructive or Marxist readings of George Eliot's novels. Rather, I have allowed these readings to influence my account of the novels without necessarily indicating this explicitly. This means that my defence of George Eliot's realism does not defend her writing as simply speaking the truth of which she writes. Rather, I offer her as a model; as a writer who, in the terms and categories available to her, attempts to understand and make sense of the social history of her time and the possibilities for individual fulfilment made available by that history.

There are, then, important issues at stake in the discussion of George Eliot's novels, issues which still have a live presence in our culture. In addition to that large issue of realism, in what follows we shall be concerned with some of the central preoccupations of the novels. They are addressed, for example, to questions of class, and to locating those forces which work for historical continuity and change. They seek to understand the relations that subsist between people in society, and how they might be improved. They tackle questions of gender, asking in particular how valid are the limits which circumscribe women's lives. I shall try to get a perspective on these questions by considering George Eliot and her work historically, by placing her in the appropriate social and historical situation. I hope in this way to understand the specific ways in which she broaches these various questions, and to assess the various solutions she offers to them. In short, in order to place ourselves fully in relation to her novels, we need to understand them in historical terms; only by understanding their location in their own time can we assess their possible importance to us across the time that now divides us from their author.

A brief word of explanation about the layout of the book before we proceed. I discuss the novels in the order in which they were written, but there is an argument which develops through the course of the book and later chapters will make more sense if you have read the earlier chapters first. There are two central strands to this argument. The first is an attempt to trace the development of the notion of the 'extension of sympathy' in the course of George Eliot's writing. I argue that this notion can best be understood in terms of class relations; the various novels consist of different ways of combining representations of the 'popular' classes, aimed at bracing the ties of sympathy that bind people together in society. This first strand is cued by the first chapter, of personal and intellectual biography, which culminates in the notion of sympathy as a crucial concept for both positivism and liberalism. The second strand of argument is a cumulative account of the novels' formal organisation. The project of the extension of sympathy presupposes a distance between author and reader, on the one hand, and the characters on the other, with important consequences for the novels' form. This book provides successively more complex ways of describing this distance, starting from evident ironies created by class and historical differences, and leading to the notion of a discursive hierarchy, which I introduce and explain in the chapter on *Middlemarch*. This notion is in turn modified in the final chapter, on *Daniel Deronda*. It requires modification because it assumes too readily that the reader can easily assess the weight to be given to the various discourses which any novel combines. *Daniel Deronda* suggests, however, that it is often difficult to assess the rhetorical impact of the different discourses of the novel, and that one of the main reasons for this, in George Eliot's case especially, is the question of gender. If, instead of the notion of a discursive hierarchy, we think in terms of a discursive economy, we are better placed to recognise the potentially unstable values that are attached above all to women's desires in the book. So the final chapter, which looks at *Daniel Deronda* from the perspective of the representation of women, is the culmination of the second strand of argument concerned with questions of form. I begin, however, with an account of George Eliot's social and intellectual formation.

1

From Marian Evans to George Eliot

I

The England of 1819 into which Mary Anne Evans was born was very different from the one she left on her death in 1880. (We shall discuss later why she adopted a pen-name.) In the first place, it was still a predominantly rural country—more people lived in the countryside than in the towns until 1850—ruled by a highly self-confident landowning class basking in its victory over revolutionary and Napoleonic France. The Industrial Revolution was still more or less confined to Lancashire, in the classic cotton towns of Manchester and its surroundings, but elsewhere in England, in the north-east, in Yorkshire and the West Midlands, in Newcastle, Leeds, Birmingham and Coventry, metropolitan and local capital were investing in the new industrial techniques that transformed England in the nineteenth century. In this process alternative centres of wealth and power arose to challenge that traditional landowning class. Both landowning and commercial classes, of course, depended upon a rural and urban working class, who exerted a continuous pressure on the classes above them—in addition to George Eliot's birth, 1819 is famous as the year of the Peterloo massacre. The pressure exerted by this working class is one highly important factor underlying the long drawn-out struggle for social and political control fought from the power bases of land and industry. Nevertheless, the various engagements, shifts and compromises of this struggle provide a central element of English history in the nineteenth century.

Mary Anne Evans' father, Robert Evans, was an important lieutenant of the landowning class in his own vicinity, for he was the agent of Francis Newdigate of Arbury Hall, near Nuneaton, Warwickshire. Though he was trained as a carpenter, his responsibilities as an agent included, in addition to general estate management (particularly of the timber), management of the mining enterprises which contributed to the Newdigate wealth. His second wife, Christiana Pearson, Mary Anne's mother, came of a yeoman family; she, her husband and her relations figure prominently in the novels, but transformed into representatives of a class—the conservative, traditional, uncultured, narrow-minded and prosperous tenantry and yeomanry of the English farming counties. Robert Evans, clearly, was a man who felt no gap between his position as landlord's agent and his understanding of that position, for he was quite comfortable in his old-fashioned Toryism and high and dry Anglicanism.

His daughter, however, sent to school first in Nuneaton and then Coventry, was caught up in the transforming religious current of Evangelicalism, a fervid, all-embracing form of belief which, during the first half of the nineteenth century, rejuvenated substantial portions of both the Anglican and Dissenting Churches. We begin to get quite a full picture of her from the age of seventeen, for a considerable quantity of her letters to her first teacher, an Evangelical Irishwoman, have survived. They are the letters of a pious and intelligent young woman, full of religious reflections, Biblical quotations, and conventional confessions of ignorance and idleness. I say these confessions are conventional because Mary Anne Evans' extraordinary capacity for assimilating knowledge is already apparent: she has learnt French and German, so, at the age of twenty, she sets herself to learn Latin and later Greek; she reads widely in a number of contemporary sciences; she even considers compiling a Chronology of early Christianity, an enterprise requiring massive diligence and minute reading (perhaps fortunately she was forestalled by another publication). She has a poem published in an Evangelical magazine, yet she combines these various self-educating projects with house-keeping for her father in a substantial farmhouse—late in life she was to attribute the large size of one of her hands to the hours she spent making butter.

The decisive event of Mary Anne Evans' life, however, was not to be her conversion to Evangelicalism, but her conversion out of it. In 1841 she moved with her father to Foleshill in Coventry, and there fell in with a group of people who had such an important effect on her life that they deserve separate description.

We have already noticed how a challenge to the rule of the English landowning class was mounted from the power centres of the industrial towns. This challenge was not only a question of power and wealth, however; it also had an ambitious cultural aspect, in which a middle-class intellectual vanguard tried both to draw on the traditional strengths of Dissent, and to capture the cultural prestige of science. The group into which Mary Anne Evans was thrown in Coventry was engaged in just such an attempt to construct a middle-class counter-culture. The Brays and the Hennells made their money out of the ribbon trade (in this they resemble the

11

Vincys and the Plymdales in *Middlemarch*, for they too, though they are 'manufacturers', put the weaving out to outworkers and run warehouses, not factories). Charles Bray, his wife Cara, and his sister-in-law Sara Hennell, were to become life-long friends of Mary Anne Evans. He was an author, free-thinker (though of a Deistical kind), phrenologist, socialist of a very utopian kind, defender of trade unionism (though not of strikes), and a leader of many local educational and philanthropic societies. He also owned and edited the liberal *Coventry Herald*, in which Mary Anne Evans published some writing in the 1840s. His brother-in-law, Charles Hennell, published in 1838 the *Origin of Christianity*, which repudiated the miraculous elements in Christianity, especially the Resurrection (it becomes a 'beautiful fiction'), and asserted that the Christian religion should be seen as 'the purest form yet existing of natural religion'. The Hennells were Unitarians, a Dissenting sect which descended from eighteenth-century Presbyterianism; unlike most other Dissenting sects they were outward-looking, rationalistic, modernising and frequently wealthy. They formed a kind of vanguard, in fact, in the attempt to construct a liberal culture; through the Hennells, Mary Anne Evans joined a connection which included not only Elizabeth Gaskell and Harriet Martineau, but a substantial body of people active in progressive middle-class thought and politics.

The result of her association with this circle (the Brays were near neighbours) was that she rapidly lost her faith, to the disgust of her father and her brother, who thought that outlandish opinions would damage her marriage prospects. It was not merely a loss of faith, though; it involved taking on a series of assumptions and attitudes not only about religion but also about man and society. Above all, it involved the belief, enunciated very clearly in Charles Bray's *The Philosophy of Necessity*, that man's social, moral and mental life were subject to law, necessity and the invariability of cause and effect in just the same way as the physical world—a belief in science, in short, as an appropriate guide through life. To embrace this belief meant not only abandoning a personal faith, it also brought with it a profound antagonism to the traditional and unsystematic ideological supports of the landowning ascendancy. The careers of Mary Anne Evans, the translator and reviewer, and of George Eliot the novelist, can be seen as extended attempts to reconstruct the ideological basis for social cohesion without the help of God or King.

Mary Anne Evans (in 1851 she began to spell her name Marian) was initiated into intellectual life, then, by a particularly ambitious and forward-looking section of the provincial middle class. Many of the ideas to which she was introduced by them she retained throughout her life; but perhaps more importantly, these ideas enabled her to assimilate the ideas of major forward-looking continental thinkers—principally the German theologian and Higher Critic of the Bible, D.F. Strauss; the humanist philosopher, Ludwig Feuerbach; and the French philosopher and architect of the Religion of Humanity, Auguste Comte. I shall discuss these men's ideas shortly, they are of the highest importance to the novels. First, let us resume the account of Marian Evans' life up to the publication of *Scenes of Clerical Life* in 1857.

Charles Hennell's book, *Origin of Christianity*, had attracted the attention of Dr R.H. Brabant, a doctor from Devizes who had some pretensions to scholarship (he is one of the possible models for Casaubon in *Middlemarch*). He was acquainted with the work of the German Higher Critics, a body of scholarship which had turned the full apparatus of historical and philological method on the Bible, with devastating results for its claims as an authentic historical record. The culmination of this body of work was D.F. Strauss's *Leben Jesu*, which, minutely and at great length,

13

examined the Biblical accounts of the life of Jesus and concluded that the New Testament records could best be explained as a myth in which the early Christians had clothed their sense of the divinity of Christ. This was the work which Dr Brabant's daughter had undertaken to translate into English. Soon after her marriage to Charles Hennell she abandoned the task to Marian Evans. It was a daunting attempt in many respects. Not only did the work require enormous industry (the book runs to 800 dense pages), but it also required a knowledge of German (of course), Latin, Greek, and occasionally some Hebrew. In addition, the idiom of German philosophy and scholarship differs widely from that of their English equivalents and this posed some nice problems of translation. In the event, she found it very heavy going—she suffered especially while translating Strauss's dissection of the various accounts of the Crucifixion—but finally succeeded. With the publication, in 1846, of *The Life of Jesus, Critically Examined* Marian Evans proved her credentials as an intellectual.

Why should the Bray-Hennell circle have been so concerned with these religious questions? In their negative or critical aspects the work of Hennell and Strauss can be seen as a kind of intellectual settling of accounts—an attempt to clear away the major outstanding obstacle to further intellectual progress. Their work was not only critical however; it can also be seen as an attempt to rescue some essential truth in Christianity, to find some basis for the moral and religious life untouched by the criticisms of science, or at least compatible with them. This was certainly the case with the next major work of philosophy which Marian Evans translated—Ludwig Feuerbach's *Essence of Christianity*. But before then her life had been transformed in a variety of ways.

In 1849, Robert Evans died, and at the age of 29 his daughter was left with a small annuity and no obvious purpose in life. Apart from the dismal prospects of teaching or governessing (compare the prospects facing Gwendolen Harleth after the failure of the family fortunes in *Daniel Deronda*), there was literally no career open to women—unless you count marriage as a career, and there were unlikely to be suitable partners for an earnest intellectual woman among her family's friends and relations in rural Warwickshire. In this situation, after a lonely year spent abroad in Geneva, she made a series of extraordinarily courageous decisions. In the first place, she decided to move to London and try to supplement her income by writing. The only other woman, to my knowledge, who made a similar decision to support herself by non-fictional, serious writing was Harriet Martineau, whose intellectual trajectory was similar in some ways to George Eliot's and whose personal life was equally courageous, if less appealing.

The milieu that Marian Evans entered in London centred on the publisher of *The Life of Jesus*, John Chapman, who also published a number of other rationalistic and forward-looking scientific books. Like the Bray–Hennell circle in Coventry, of which indeed this was a metropolitan equivalent, this milieu brought together the leaders of English liberal culture. Chapman published the *Westminster Review*, a journal with a proud intellectual history on the Radical side. (Radical is an important word in George Eliot's career—the title of one of her books, after all, is *Felix Holt, the Radical*. Here, however, I use it to mean a specifically political position which seeks to rationalise the political order by making it more democratic and by ridding it of conservative and traditional anomalies and abuses.) Marian Evans soon became effective editor of the *Review* in addition to writing substantial contributions for it. This position brought her into contact with an advanced section of the middle-class intelligentsia; it marked her own ability to live as an independent intellectual expecting to be paid for her writing.

15

One of the most important figures of this milieu was Herbert Spencer, an understanding of whose work is very useful in understanding George Eliot's novels; I shall discuss it shortly. He and Marian Evans became so familiar that she had to discount rumours that they were engaged to be married. Another important figure was the journalist, philosopher and man of letters, George Henry Lewes. Meeting him led to another important decision—to live together. The decision was courageous because the marriage could not be a legal one, since Lewes was already married. It was this connection with Lewes which was soon to lead to the creation of George Eliot.

It is hard to overestimate the difficulties encumbering such a relationship in mid-nineteenth-century England, despite the fact that there was clearly no wrong involved to Lewes's wife. (She already had two children by Thornton Hunt, a Radical journalist and colleague of Lewes's on the *Leader* newspaper, and was to have two more.) Divorce was impossible since Lewes had apparently condoned his wife's adultery. To live openly with a man not your husband meant social ostracism for the woman, though thanks to the Victorian double-standard, not for the man. For Marian Evans it meant being cut off from her family—her brother Isaac Evans was especially harsh, refusing to write to her during the 24 years of her union with Lewes, and then congratulating her on her marriage to John Cross a few months before her death in 1880. (He also had the effrontery to appear as a chief mourner at her funeral.) It meant deciding to have no children of their own, especially as Lewes was already responsible for three children by his legal wife, whom he continued to maintain with her children until his death. It meant above all an effective isolation from ordinary social contact; it was only at the end of their lives together that Lewes and George Eliot became possible, even desirable, visitors and friends in middle-class drawing rooms.

Unsurprisingly in these circumstances, they at first contemplated living much of their time abroad. In the event, they were to be indefatigable travellers.

Lewes himself, as I have suggested, was a considerable intellectual and writer in his own right. The author of a *Biographical History of Philosophy*, a novel, several plays, innumerable substantial articles in the reviews in addition to his work-a-day journalism, he also performed professionally as an actor. After writing an account of Comte's *Positive Philosophy*, which was criticised by Huxley as being written by a 'book-scientist', he turned himself into a genuine, practical physiologist. His most celebrated contribution, however, was the first English (or indeed German) biography of Goethe, which he published in 1855, one year after starting his life with Marian Evans. He was very much the senior intellectual partner in the relationship when it began in 1854; it was his encouragement and support, both at the beginning and throughout their life together, which was to overcome her habitual diffidence about her writing and which provided her with an environment in which her novels could be written.

The position of Lewes and Marian Evans in the mid-1850s, then, the time when George Eliot was created, was a very interesting one. Thanks to the irregularity of their marriage, they were placed at a position slightly askew to the society in which they lived; yet both were engaged on intellectual tasks absolutely central to the problems of mid-nineteenth-century Britain—principally the construction of a secular and scientifically acceptable ideological basis for that social formation. It is in this sense that their status as 'intellectuals' is to be understood—not merely as learned people who earned their living by their writing, but people whose work was addressed to some of the crucial problems of their time and their class. (It is significant that one of the few uses of the word 'intellectual' in the mid-nineteenth century—the word and the concept only came into general currency at the end of the century—should be in one of George Eliot's letters for 1852.) We need to get a better sense of just what these problems were, and we can best do so by considering the work of the various writers with whom Marian Evans felt a substantial affinity.

II

Let us begin with Ludwig Feuerbach, whose *Essence of Christianity* she translated in 1854—the only book ever to appear under her own name. Feuerbach is an infinitely more interesting and appealing philosopher than Strauss, though it is indicative of the state of English culture in the mid-century that it should have been the latter's minute Biblical scholarship which gained an audience rather than Feuerbach's bold and witty speculations: the translation fell stillborn from the press. The central argument of the book is briefly stated. It attempts to invert or unveil the essential truths of religion, so that the attributes of God stand revealed for what they really are: the attributes of Man. The divine attributes of Reason, Will and Affection are really no more than projections of Man's own highest and species-specific characteristics. Feuerbach's atheism is thus very different from the merely negative atheism of the eighteenth century. It is a 'religious atheism', a humanism which seeks to return to human, social and material life the aspect of sanctity which dogmatic religion robs from it. 'The relation of child and parent,' he writes, 'of husband and wife, of brother and friend—in general, of man to man—in short all the moral relations are *per se* religious. Life as a whole is, in its essential, substantial relations, throughout of a divine nature.'[1] The book is thus a joyful and even celebratory one. It provides a way of thinking about religion which is fundamentally positive because religion stands revealed as a mistaken

18

objectification of man's own highest, subjective, yearnings and feelings.

The appeal of such a book to the translator of *Life of Jesus* is apparent. Still more important is its appeal to Marian Evans the middle-class intellectual. For here was the intellectual basis which could enable the middle class—rapidly becoming dominant in English social life—to assimilate and integrate the ideology which helped to justify the rule of the previous dominant class. She need no longer consider religion merely as an obstacle and as a negative social force; she need no longer cut herself off from much of the national life and from her own past; she now has grounds for assimilating religion into the wider and indeed progressive life of humanity.

Feuerbachian conceptions are to be found throughout George Eliot's novels, but especially in the early ones. *Adam Bede* in particular can be called a Feuerbachian novel in the strict sense; for just as Feuerbach considered that his work was 'a *translation* of the Christian religion out of the Oriental language of imagery into plain speech',[2] so can the religious language of the novel be translated into the language of humanism. Consider, for example, this description of Dinah Morris as she is about to preach: 'There was no keenness in the eyes; they seemed rather to be shedding love than making observations; they had the liquid look which tells that the mind is full of what it has to give out, rather than impressed by external objects' (*Adam Bede*, ch.2). You might think of this merely as a heightened description of someone in a state of concentration; but it is much more than this, for this attitude accurately expresses the Feuerbachian truth that the source of sanctity or divine inspiration is to be found within, in a person's subjective capacity for love, affection or feeling: 'The divine nature which is discerned by feeling,' he writes, 'is in truth nothing else than feeling enraptured, in ecstasy with itself—feeling intoxicated with joy, blissful in its own plenitude'.[3] The comparison with Dinah is striking.

More generally, however, Feuerbach is interesting not because he enables us to make these immediate comparisons, but because he enables George Eliot to assimilate religion—in this case, Methodism—to the onward progress of humanity. She does so however, in a way which tends to strip religion of any disruptive or socially challenging aspects. The Feuerbachian saints who inhabit George Eliot's novels—Tryan, Dinah Morris, Maggie Tulliver, Romola, Felix Holt, Dorothea Brooke, Mordecai—all, with the possible exception of the last, inspire to submission rather than revolt. In doing so they are representing another aspect of George Eliot's thought, in which the itegrationist, non-disruptive, even conservative elements of her intellectual position are uppermost. For these aspects of her thought it is helpful to turn to Herbert Spencer and Auguste Comte.

I have been suggesting that the intellectual development of Marian Evans can be understood as part of a general attempt to construct a middle-class, anti-aristocratic culture based on a belief in science and drawing on the traditions of Nonconformity and Dissent. There was, of course, a conservative aspect to this project, involving a repudiation of rapid or revolutionary political change, a commitment to the laws of the market and the current division of labour, and even, in extreme form, a rejection of politics as such. A dual project, in fact, embracing both the necessity for change and the necessity for that change to be ordered and to come from the internal dynamics of society itself—a dual project summed up in the Comtist slogan, 'Order and Progress'. This slogan, for all its generality, precisely captures both the positive and negative aspects characterising the ideological needs of the mid-nineteenth-century middle class.

The works of both Herbert Spencer and Auguste Comte represent ambitious attempts to provide an intellectual synthesis which could adequately ground this dual project.

The intellectual tradition within which both worked (though there were, of course, important differences between their two positions) can best be described as positivist, a word coined by Comte himself to designate adherence to a belief in positive science, namely, knowledge which can demonstrate invariable sequence and succession in the phenomena with which it deals, while eschewing any pretence to explain ultimate causes. For both thinkers, science thus understood was to found a science of society which would both demonstrate the laws of social development (social dynamics), and establish the limits within which all societies must live, and with this make apparent the limits to all variation and change (social statics). For Herbert Spencer the most appropriate scientific analogy for this conception of society was provided by biology. Society was to be conceived as an organism, which evolved in the manner of organic beings thanks to the action and interaction of its internal constitution with its environment.

This is a powerful, and in many ways a luminous, conception. It immediately enables you to examine society as such; it provides you with an object of study. And it strikingly suggests the interdependence of the various members of society, whose different functions can be seen as the various organs of a body. The shortcomings of such a conception need stressing as well, however. It tends to consecrate the actually existing. For Spencer in particular, this meant that the laws of the market and the division of labour were permanently secured by being the essential processes by which the social organism continued. In addition, to conceive of society in this organicist way meant that historical changes or improvements can only be sanctioned if they are adaptive, incremental, growing out of the already existent. It is in this sense that George Eliot was to describe herself as a 'meliorist'.

For society and social change are conceived in this

organicist way throughout George Eliot's novels. A whole series of organic metaphors—of veins and arteries, of fibres, roots, and webs—are deployed to carry this conception both of the way people are linked together in society, and of the way the present is linked to the past. When, for example, in *Mill on the Floss*, George Eliot writes of the 'oppressive narrowness' which 'has acted on young natures in many generations, that in the onward tendency of human things have risen above the mental level of the generation before them, to which they have been nevertheless tied by the strongest fibres of their hearts' (*The Mill on the Floss*, IV, 1), you have an especially clear example of organicist thought. The 'oppressive narrowness' (of the Dodsons and the Tullivers, in this case) acts as an internal social constraint which propels the young natures to act, according to their nature, in a way which transforms the social organism; but the transformation means that the organism remains recognisably the same because of the 'fibrous' links of the present to the past.

Once again, however, the point is not merely to identify examples of organicist thought in George Eliot's writing but to see that by propelling such thought through her novels she is engaged in an intellectual project which takes its dynamic from central problems of the mid-nineteenth century. Nor do her novels simply represent a collage of other people's thought; rather they make their own intellectual contribution, being a synthesis in which this body of thought is rethought in the formal means appropriate to the novel.

Comte, like Spencer, attempted to place contemporary society in an evolutionary series, though he felt that when social knowledge was everywhere acknowledged to have reached a state of positivity, and when society could be held together by the Religion of Humanity which would replace the old religions, then that evolutionary series would come to an end, for the full meaning and purpose of human history would have been realised. Like Spencer's, Comte's work represents a synthesis of massive ambition. For G.H. Lewes he was, quite simply, 'the greatest thinker of modern times'.[4] He began by classifying the sciences in a way which was both historically and theoretically based, for he arranged them in a sequence which showed how each science, starting with mathematics and ending with his own invention, 'sociology', had reached a positive state in an historical order but based on their increasing complexity. Throughout, he insisted that positive knowledge meant certainty of succession, and that knowledge could never be more than this certainty that the same causes invariably produce the same results. Each individual science, like human history itself, had to pass through the preceding theological and metaphysical (negative) stages, before it reached a positive state. The theological stage of knowledge itself comprised three phases, in which men, in attempting to explain their world, began by attributing volitions like their own to inanimate objects (fetishism), proceeded to generalise these various phenomena into comparative groups (polytheism), and finally recognised the invariable action of uniform power throughout the universe (monotheism). The metaphysical state which succeeded the theological was understood to mean the critical and revolutionary spirit of the eighteenth century which culminated in the French Revolution. Comte saw his task as providing the intellectual and even religious basis for a new order which would succeed the revolutionary upheavals of his century.

This scheme had enormous appeal in mid-nineteenth-century England, not only to G.H. Lewes and George Eliot, but also to J.S. Mill, and a number of friends of George Eliot like Richard Congreve and Frederic Harrison who became convinced positivists. But Comte went much further than this scientific and historical classification; he used it to form the basis of a positivist policy, and even a carefully detailed

23

Religion of Humanity with its own tightly planned cultus. (George Eliot's hymn 'O May I Join the Choir Invisible' came to be used in the positivist rite.) In a world ruled by invariable sequence and succession, the prime individual and social duty was submission. However, such general submission could only be achieved if positive political science, and all other means of social education, had achieved general recognition of social limits. This is only possible, moreover, given a rigid separation of the theoretical and the practical, for a recognition of the true and the right must always precede political action, and indeed be uncontaminated by it. A good example of what a positivist 'political' programme would look like (it's effectively an anti-political position) is provided by Felix Holt's 'Address to Working-Men'. George Eliot wrote it at her publisher's request after the passage of the Second Reform Bill in 1867. Felix Holt here tells his fellow workmen that 'we have seriously to consider this outside wisdom which lies in the supreme unalterable nature of things, and watch to give it a home within us and obey it'.[5] Submission to the necessary, guided by the wisdom of those who can reveal it, was a cardinal principle of George Eliot's writing.

But Comte's relevance to George Eliot is greater than this. For him, 'the chief problem of human life was the subordination of egoism to altruism'.[6] Like Spencer, he conceived of human society in an evolutionary way—it is a long history leading from savage independence to mutuality and sociality. The necessarily social conditions of modern life mean that for each individual the egoistic impulses have to be subordinated to the altruistic impulses—the more the individual is capable of doing this, the more he or she advances him or herself, thus advancing society and creating the conditions for further individual and social advance. The moral evolution of the individual, therefore, is inextricable from that individual's social environment and inextricably

24

acts and reacts upon it. Not that each individual is to be understood as a blank sheet or *tabula rasa*. Individuals are born with hereditary endowments which sum up the progressive achievements of their nationality or race; and they also have differing capacities or faculties (for altruism, activity, affection, etc.) which can be strengthened or weakened by education, but which necessarily make for some degree of internal conflict. Nevertheless, the history of each individual recapitulates the history of the race; children, like savages and workmen who demonstrate some of the same characteristics, have to be educated into morality and altruism.

The joint histories of Maggie and Tom Tulliver, in *Mill on the Floss*, provide excellent examples of these various conceptions and of some of the difficulties they entail. The expansive two first volumes of the novel are extended accounts of their moral education, showing how the interaction between their own capacities and their environment creates the individuals who behave in the ways that they do in the third volume. Thus Tom, the Dodson-like son, practical, rigid and unimaginative, fits well with his environment, despite the mistaken efforts of Stelling to educate him against his natural bent. He feels little internal conflict because his loyalties and ambitions are so bound up with the Dodson world that, though capable of renovating that world materially (he is the Tamer of Horses), he is incapable of conceiving any other. Maggie, on the other hand, affectionate and imaginative, similarly has her moral nature rooted in the associations that gather round her childhood; unlike Tom, however, there is no appropriate outlet for her capacities in her environment. Her heroic efforts to subdue her egoistic impulses, culminating in the renunciation of Stephen Guest, provide a model of moral growth which, given that human history is the history of the gradual subordination of egoism to altruism, is the condition of social

25

growth. The book is thus a tragedy, but in two senses. It is the tragedy of Maggie's suffering, of the slow pace of social and moral progress whose instigators are likely to be its victims; and it is also the tragedy of a society where the practical and the affective, the just and the imaginative, cannot be reconciled except when the normal conditions of the Dodson environment are temporarily suspended in the brief interruption of the flood.

The way that George Eliot conceives of the relationship between the individual and society, then, as well as problems of social and historical change, is congruous with a substantial and developed body of thought which draws on English, French and German traditions but which offers the possibility of a real synthesis. To describe George Eliot as a positivist need not therefore imply that she strictly adhered to the views of any of the writers I have described; but it does imply her adherence to the general way of conceiving the world and society that these writers shared. Novels, however, are very different things from textbooks of sociology or psychology; rather different, too, from history books. Even the brief account I have just given of *Mill on the Floss* draws on an aesthetic category, 'tragedy', and is not given exclusively in positivist terms. George Eliot obviously draws on other sources, literary, popular and personal, in her writing. When she talks of Maggie and Tom's moral nature being rooted in the associations that gather round their childhood, this account of their development has strong Wordsworthian overtones. (The appeal of Wordsworth to George Eliot is evident throughout her writing. Her taste in this matter is not arbitrary, however, for Wordsworth's psychology derives from the same Associationist tradition that later produced Herbert Spencer.) Moreover, the shape of the novels—and *Mill on the Floss* in particular—is also determined by a mass of personal and autobiographical material which has been transformed in various ways but which is still powerfully present. If the resort to the novel form can in part be explained by the need to represent and give coherence to this other material, the question still remains: why write novels, instead of giving us positivism straight? To answer this question takes us to the heart of George Eliot's art.

First, that art is a didactic art. There is never any question, from the beginning to the end of her career as a novelist, but that George Eliot sought to educate her readers; and we are reminded that in a world ruled by the invariable succession of cause and effect, education is one of the few possible kinds of intervention open to the positivist intellectual. She sought to educate her readers by the whole range of techniques available to the novelist—by example, by generalising from her narratives, by providing models of behaviour that would reinforce positive tendencies, by showing the sometimes unexpected consequences of unhealthy habits and beliefs. Her capacity to lend generality or typicality to characters and narrative is crucial in this respect, as is her perceived relationship to her readership. George Eliot's novels are a committed intervention in the social life of mid-nineteenth-century England.

Secondly, the kind of education provided by novels is especially appropriate in the attempt to subordinate egoism to altruism. Even without overt didactism, novels can teach, in a famous phrase of hers, the 'extension of our sympathies', and thus their great responsibility to provide unsentimental representations, so that the reader's sympathies can be extended in ways which will not be disappointed. Sympathy is an absolutely crucial concept throughout George Eliot's writing. It provides the very basis upon which society is possible, for it is the emotional aspect of the social feelings which the progress of society more and more calls into play. Sympathy, in short, is a kind of social cement, and it is to the extension of our sympathies, to their education and direction, that the novels are addressed. The centrality of this notion to

27

the intellectual concerns of the mid-century can be gauged from a comparison with J.S. Mill's *Utilitarianism* (1863), with likewise identifies sympathy as an essential agent in the formation and strengthening of social feelings. For Mill too, the central problem was how to provide intellectual grounds for the conversion of egoistic into altruistic impulses; though George Eliot was never a utilitarian, her novels, as novels, centre on this problem, and indeed seek to provide part of the solution to it in the very fact of being read.

Finally, the novel allows George Eliot scope for an imaginative power kept in check by writing constrained by other conventions for getting access to the real. Imagination was another central notion for George Eliot. Late in her career she gave this striking description of it:

> powerful imagination is not false outward vision, but intense inward representation, and a creative energy constantly fed by susceptibility to the veriest minutiae of experience, which it reproduces and constructs in fresh and fresh wholes; not the habitual confusion of provable fact with the fictions of fancy and transient inclination, but a breadth of ideal association which informs every material object, every incidental fact with far-reaching memories and stored residues of passion, bringing into new light the less obvious relations of human existence. (*Theophrastus Such*, 'How we come to give ourselves false testimonials, and believe in them')

Imagination here is emphatically not a flight from reality but a capacity for further penetration into it. The freedom of an imaginative form like the novel thus brings with it great opportunities for exposing unthought of relations, new connections charged with the affective power of passion; but it also brings heavy responsibilities that these 'fresh and fresh wholes' should be compatible with the real. George Eliot's novels are certainly to be fictions, but they are fictions that are true.

'George Eliot' was created early in 1857, 'as a tub to throw to the whale in case of curious inquiries', she wrote to her publisher still in ignorance of her real identity. 'George was Mr Lewes' Christian name, and Eliot was a good mouth-filling easily-pronouncced word.'[7] A lot is hidden, however, behind these flippant-sounding explanations. Marian Evans needed a pen-name for several reasons: she wanted to ensure that the novels were judged on their merits, and not as the novels of the scandalous translater of Strauss and Feuerbach, nor as the still more scandalous consort of George Henry Lewes; she needed to protect her own position and her family's, for all the early novels were to contain much local and personal history; and she also wished to ensure, as Charlotte Brontë had done ten years earlier by publishing under the name of Currer Bell, that the novels were judged irrespective of the sex of the author—reviewers then still more than now judging 'women's writing' by false standards. Quite how George Eliot managed the various problems assimilated by Marian Evans we shall discuss in the following chapters.

2

'The Extension of Our Sympathies'

I

I have suggested the central importance of 'sympathy' to George Eliot's understanding of social life. It is such an important notion for her that this chapter is devoted to considering the implications of the doctrine of sympathy, especially in her first four novels; at the end of the chapter I suggest some reservations about the idea.

Let us begin by considering the substantial passage, written before she embarked on *Scenes of Clerical Life*, where she connects the notion of sympathy to art, and links it with the questions of class and artistic realism. The passage occurs in an essay written for the *Westminster Review* in 1855, called 'The Natural History of German Life'; it can be read as a remarkable aesthetic manifesto:

> our social novels profess to represent the people as they are, and
> the unreality of their representations is a grave evil. The greatest
> benefit we owe to the artist, whether painter, poet, or novelist, is

the extension of our sympathies. Appeals founded on generalisations and statistics require a sympathy ready-made, a moral sentiment already in activity; but a picture of human life such as a great artist can give, surprises even the trivial and the selfish into that attention into what is apart from themselves, which may be called the raw material of moral sentiment. When Scott takes us into Luckie Mucklebackit's cottage, or tells the story of The Two Drovers—when Wordsworth sings to us the reverie of 'Poor Susan',—when Kingsley shows us Alton Locke gazing yearningly over the gate which leads from the highway into the first wood he ever saw,—when Hornung paints a group of chimney-sweepers,—more is done towards linking the higher classes with the lower, towards obliterating the vulgarity of exclusiveness, than by hundreds of sermons and philosophical dissertations. Art is the nearest thing to life; it is a mode of amplifying experience and extending our contact with our fellow-men beyond the bounds of our personal lot. All the more sacred is the task of the artist when he undertakes to paint the life of the People. Falsification here is far more pernicious than in the more artificial aspects of life. It is not so very serious that we should have false ideas about evanescent fashions—about the manners and conversations of beaux and duchesses; but it *is* serious that our sympathy with the perennial joys and struggles, the toil, the tragedy, and the humour in the life of our more heavily-laden fellow-men, should be perverted, and turned towards a false object instead of the true one.

This perversion is not the less fatal because the misrepresentation which gives rise to it has what the artist considers a moral end. The thing for mankind to know is, not what are the motives and influences which ought to act on the labourer or the artisan, but what are the motives and influences which *do* act on him. We want to be taught to feel, not for the heroic artisan or the sentimental peasant, but for the peasant in all his coarse apathy and the artisan in all his suspicious selfishness.[1]

Several distinct ideas are strikingly linked together in this powerful passage. There is the overarching view of society held together by sympathy, which provides the basis for morality. In the light of this conception, the artist has a responsibility to provide unsentimental and verifiable representations of 'the people' because art has a direct effect on people's sympathies and thus on the way people relate to each other in society. Reading this passage as a manifesto illuminates all George Eliot's novels, but especially *Scenes of Clerical Life* (1857), *Adam Bede* (1859), *The Mill on the Floss* (1860) and *Silas Marner* (1861). In all these novels, George Eliot is attempting to provide just that unsentimental representation of 'the people' whose absence she is deprecating. The point of doing so, in effect, is to extend the sympathies of a reader in order to bolster and maintain the bonds of social cohesion.

This is an artistic project, then, which seeks to link together the very experience of reading with the reader's relation to society; and in doing so it provides both an account of art which claims to explain what it essentially is, and criterion for measuring what it ought to be. Formulating her project in this way enables George Eliot to link her novels with the whole programme of positivism as it is directed to the overcoming of egoism by altruism. Similarly, the notion of realism that she combines with the extension of sympathy is compatible with a positivist understanding of science, where one's first obligation is to a minute and unflinching veracity and honesty in observation. It is an artistic project, in short, which locates a coherent view of art in a coherent view of nature and social life.

Throughout the early novels there is a consistent attempt to stress the community of experience between reader, character and narrator, despite the superficial differences of class and historical distance that appear to separate them. Whether it be the tenant-farmers and artisans of *Adam Bede*, the Dodsons and Tullivers of *The Mill on the Floss*, or the rustics of Raveloe in *Silas Marner*, as readers we are to sympathise with those aspects of their lives which make up their 'perennial joys and struggles', at least if we are reading the novels in the spirit which George Eliot desires. In reading the novels thus sympathetically we will be adding to or extending our moral faculties in ways which will qualify us for moral solidarity with our fellow men and women.

This way of conceiving the moral and social relations between people, as being based on a fundamental ground of sympathy more secure than superficial differences, is so prevalent in George Eliot's thinking that it informs not only the way she conceives of her books being read, but also repeatedly appears within the novels as the basis for the relations between characters. Sympathy, 'the one poor word which includes all our best insight and our best love' (*Adam Bede*, ch.50), is constantly mobilised within the novels to break down barriers between people; the capacity for sympathy is the main indication of moral nobility. Thus in the climactic scene of *Adam Bede*, when Dinah Morris meets the unrepentant Hetty Sorrel in prison in hopes of making her confess to the murder of her child, it is the enormous power of Dinah's sympathy, understood by both as the pity of Jesus, which melts the hard shell of Hetty's vanity and moral stupidity. In a less exalted context, and indeed a less theologically loaded one, Mr Tulliver in *The Mill on the Floss* shows how sympathy for one person can become the basis for sympathy for another, much as the reader's sympathies for the characters of a novel can be converted into the sympathy for real men and women. He forbears pressing his sister for the return of a loan because he imagines that he would not like Tom to be hard on Maggie: 'this was his confused way of explaining to himself that his love and anxiety for "the little wench" had given him a new sensibility towards his sister' (*The Mill on the Floss*, I, 8). Instances of this sort abound in the novels; as a final example consider how, in *Silas Marner*, human sympathy conceived in this way

33

is the very essence of the fable; for it is Silas's sympathy with Eppie which leads to his regenerated relation with society and the world.

However, what is striking about the passage from 'The Natural History of German Life' is the way that sympathy is insistently linked to questions of class. It is class above all which provides the main barrier preventing the flow of sympathy from the reader. We can see this immediately if we ask whose sympathies are to be extended. The answer is clearly the middle-class readership of the *Westminster Review*, a readership which is presupposed in this passage but which is cognate with the readership presupposed in a multiplicity of ways in the novels as well. Throughout the passage, the middle-class reader is a spectator on working-class or peasant experience. All of the examples, from Scott, Wordsworth, Kingsley and the genre painter Hornung, provide typical or exemplary moments of popular life. The project of 'the extension of our sympathies' is precisely directed against the 'vulgarity of exclusiveness'—that kind of mentality which seeks to maintain the distinctions of class, and whose most trivial but also most pervasive manifestation is snobbishness; while the project is directed towards social cohesiveness understood in class terms, as 'linking the higher classes with the lower'.

This artistic project, then, appears to be a directly egalitarian one. It can be compared to the aesthetic (or way of conceiving and judging art) outlined in Wordsworth's 'Preface' to the *Lyrical Ballads* (1800), which similarly sought to found an egalitarian art on the 'primary laws of our nature', and which chose 'low and rustic life' to demonstrate those laws because here human nature was less overlaid with the artifices of society. George Eliot resembles Wordsworth also in accompanying this assertion of a fundamental humanity with a rejection of 'artificial' writing, conceived as appealing to a spoilt and aristocratic taste. This whole nexus of ideas, while obviously put together with very different emphases by Wordsworth and George Eliot, is nevertheless a characteristically bourgeois combination. It links the 'extension of our sympathies' with realism, asserts the intrinsic value of writing about 'the people', and rejects artificial or aristocratic genres. In articulating this powerful combination of ideas and feelings, George Eliot is making explicit the rationale for what has become the dominant form of the novel—realism—with her own novels providing decisive examples. We shall return to the questions raised by the term realism; here let us note how this structure of feeling, expressed with different emphases, is important also in the work of George Eliot's contemporary novelists Mrs Gaskell, W.M. Thackeray, and, more intermittently, Charles Dickens.

To whom, however, are 'our' sympathies to be extended in the early novels? The answer is perhaps more complicated, and less unreservedly popular, than either the passage from 'The Natural History of German Life' or the comparable passage from *Adam Bede*, would suggest. In Chapter 17 of that novel, 'in which the story pauses a little', we are given another powerful defence of realism:

> But let us love that other beauty, too, which lies in no secret of proportion, but in the secret of deep human sympathy. Paint us an angel, if you can ... paint us yet oftener a Madonna ...
> but do not impose on us any aesthetic rules which shall banish from the region of Art those old women scraping carrots with their work-worn hands, those heavy clowns taking holiday in a dingy pot-house, those rounded backs and stupid weather-beaten faces that have bent over the spade and done the rough work of the world, those houses with their tin pans, their brown pitchers, their rough curs and their clusters of onions. (*Adam Bede*, ch. 17)

This has a wonderful solidity of detail, but it is little more than a rhetorical flourish in the novel as a whole, for it is certainly not to carrot-scraping women or heavy clowns that we are most drawn in *Adam Bede*, or for that matter in any of George Eliot's novels. Indeed, she finds it persistently difficult to represent such people sympathetically, finding their 'stupidity' and resistance to higher motives, however explicable, a heavy clog on the onward processes of social life. No, it is not to these people that the dominant movement of sympathy is expressed; it is to classes decidedly more respectable, in whose daily habits and values she can find evidence of the growing good of the world. Thus, in the opening scene of *Adam Bede* in the carpenters' shop, the reader is to sympathise, obviously enough, with Adam himself rather than with Wiry Ben. Adam's hands are certainly 'work-worn', but for him work is a kind of vocation: 'I hate to see a man's arms drop down as if he was shot, before the clock's fairly struck, just as if he'd never a bit o'pride and delight in's work' (*Adam Bede*, ch.1). Similarly, George Eliot carefully commemorates the labourers on the Poyser farm in the 'Harvest Supper' chapter of *Adam Bede*, again repudiating the 'picturesque' which makes the world seem prettier than it really is. But it is to their employers, the Poysers themselves, that the main current of sympathy runs in the novel as a whole. There is thus at least an ambivalence in the notion of the 'popular' as it is used by George Eliot to justify her artistic practice, for it covers a split within the non-aristocratic classes. On the one hand, she wishes to assert the artistic worth and dignity of the 'hard-handed' (though in doing so she is not far from providing her own version of the picturesque—'You and I are indebted to the hard hands of such men—hands that have long ago mingled with the soil they tilled so faithfully, thriftily making the best they could of the earth's fruits, and receiving the smallest share as their own wages' (*Adam Bede*, ch. 17)). On the other hand, the main current of the novels runs with the more prudent, vocationally hard-working and middle-class segments above them.

Despite this necessary qualification, however, it is still clear that George Eliot characteristically chooses, as central objects of the reader's sympathies, people and classes who have previously been excluded from the ambit of novelistic sympathy, either because they have been thought too dull to merit novelistic representation (itself a disguised class judgement), or because they have been habitually represented in picturesque or idealising ways. This situation has important consequences within the novels. Since George Eliot is struggling against prejudice, propelled in other writing and in other fictions, her own fictions are in effect competing against other representations; she has constantly to justify both the worth and the authenticity of the representations she is providing. The meanings of her novels in part emerge from these differences from previous writing.

Consider, for example, the following passage from *Scenes of Clerical Life*, which could be matched by a number of comparable passages in all the early novels:

The Rev. Amos Barton, whose sad fortunes I have undertaken to relate, was, you perceive, in no respect an ideal or exceptional character; and perhaps I am doing a bold thing to bespeak your sympathy on behalf of a man who was so very far from remarkable,—a man whose virtues were not heroic, and who had no undetected crime within his breast; who had not the slightest mystery hanging about him, but who was palpably and unmistakably commonplace; who was not even in love, but had had that complaint favourably many years ago. 'An utterly uninteresting character!' I think I hear a lady reader exclaim—Mrs Farthingale, for example, who prefers the ideal in fiction; to whom tragedy means ermine tippets, adultery, and murder; and comedy, the adventures of some personage who is quite a 'character'. ('The Sad Fortunes of the Rev. Amos Barton', ch. 5)

The writer here (it is not quite 'George Eliot', and not only

37

because the pen-name was yet to be invented) is clearly acutely conscious of the pressure of other ways of writing fiction, or other genres, weighing upon the fiction. The man of heroic virtues, or with an undetected crime, is the hero of another novel; tragedy and comedy understood in the way Mrs Farthingale understands them have become vicious because their aristocratic pretentiousness, or indeed their idealism, direct the reader's sympathies away from the this-worldly, the ordinary and the popular towards which they ought more properly to flow. The writer is having to work hard to justify his or her own artistic practice; the story of the Rev. Amos Barton does not just speak for itself, but has to be advanced towards its readership (predominantly genteel) by way of frequent explanatory and justificatory passages of this kind.

To be sure, this is a very early story, George Eliot's first, and in later novels she will be much more able to rely on the very prestige of her own writing to provide an authority which will not need this kind of justification. Nevertheless, even in this early passage we can see the presence of two attitudes which mark all the early novels. There is both an almost apologetic deference to a readership understood as being potentially hostile to the representation provided—this is the tone of 'perhaps I am doing a bold thing to bespeak your sympathy'; and there is also, in an almost contradictory way, a readiness to use the very commonplaceness of the representation as a source of ironies *against* the genteel reader: it is not for nothing that the 'lady reader' is named Mrs Farthingale, after the cumbrous and artifical hooped garment of aristocratic fashion. Let us look first at this latter aspect, at the way the insistence upon community of experience can be used as a source of irony against the would-be exclusive reader.

In the four early books ('successive phases of my mental life', George Eliot later called them) the location of community of experience among widely different classes in widely different times provides opportunities for different kinds of irony. In *Scenes of Clerical Life*, the insistence upon the commonplace and even the dingy (in 'Janet's Repentance' the heroine tipples) serves as a constant challenge to the reader, especially the 'lady reader', not to discount this fiction as beneath her. There is equally an irony of historical distance, for the *Scenes* are set 'more than a quarter of a century' before their date of publication. They demonstrate the regenerative effects of sympathy, pity and suffering, as applicable then as now. You cannot, therefore, simply rely on the external improvements to the town of Milby as indicative of genuine progress: 'In short, Milby is now a refined, moral and enlightened town . . .', and we are alerted not to believe it.

This irony of historical distance is perhaps more pronounced in *Adam Bede*, set at the turn of the century some 60 years before the novel was published. Again, the reader is challenged to find resemblance and community of experience beneath the distracting differences of costume, manners, speech and class. However,this does not amount to a simply conservative assertion of there being nothing new under the sun; the reader is challenged to see in what essential respects humanity might be said to progress, and to disregard superficial changes, especially of fashion or refinement. This is emphatically the case with regard to Methodism in the novel. Representations of Methodism in the first half of the nineteenth century had been overwhelmingly hostile, and the pressure of this bad press can be felt in this defensive comment: 'It is too possible that to some of my readers Methodism may mean nothng more than low-pitched gables up dirty streets, sleek grocers, sponging preachers and hypocritical jargon—elements which are regarded as an exhaustive analysis of Methodism in many fashionable quarters' (*Adam Bede* ch. 3). However, as I suggested in the Introduction, Dinah's Methodism is one of the vehicles of the divine in the novel, that is to say of the human. In so far as the reader is led to recognise this, then those class-based prejudices should tumble to the ground; and perhaps with them those gender-based prejudices which find women as unlikely a channel as Methodism for the flow of the spirit.

In *The Mill on the Floss*, however, the balance of irony, either against the reader or the characters, is tilted more strongly towards irony against the characters. We can of course find a similar rhetoric employed, as in *Adam Bede*, against the comfortable modern assumptions of the reader. Maggie Tulliver, for example, is clearly affected by Stephen Guest's admiring glances: 'Such things could have had no perceptible effect on a thoroughly well-educated young lady with a perfectly balanced mind, who had had all the advantages of fortune, training and refined society' (*The Mill on the Floss*, VI, 3). This irony against the refined reader, however, is not the dominant direction of the irony in this novel. Far more typical is a real unease about the reception of the representations being offered. There is a profound anxiety that the life of the Dodsons and Tullivers would prove so unattractive that no reader could possibly sympathise with their joys and struggles. This is most evident in the famous chapter entitled 'A Variation of Protestantism Unknown to Bossuet'; but one can equally see some anxiety about the gentility of Maggie. The irony of the passage I have just quoted depends upon the fact that Maggie is *not* a 'thoroughly well-educated young lady', but that this does not matter because in the more important fundamentals of life she is thoroughly deserving of a reader's sympathies. Nevertheless a few pages later, the Miss Guests are wondering 'that there was no tinge of vulgarity about her'; and while of course the irony operates against the Miss Guests for their small-town snobbery, it does remain the case that there *is* no vulgarity about Maggie and that this is important if she is to retain the reader's sympathies.

More generally, when, in talking of the 'emmet-like Dodsons and Tullivers', George Eliot writes that 'You could not live among such people; you are stifled for want of an outlet towards something beautiful, great or noble; you are irritated with these dull men and women, as a kind of population out of keeping with the earth on which they live' (*The Mill on the Floss*, IV, 1), there is little irony that I can detect. The only outlet to grandeur will be found in the observer's mind, not in the life of the dull men and women themselves—'there is nothing petty to the mind that has a large vision of relations.' This unease can equally be traced in the constant uncertainty about what kind of a novel this is. Is it a tragedy or a tragi-comedy? The action of Maggie's history as a child lacks the magnitude of tragedy, we are told (I,9); though later in the novel there is a classic assertion of bourgeois realism when a claim is made for the tragedy of 'millers and other insignificant people' (II,1)—in this case, Mr Tulliver. In other words the novel shows evidence of two contradictory impulses. On the one hand, there is the impulse of the scientific, classificatory mind, 'with a large vision of relations', towards providing a natural history of provincial life; from this perspective the actions of the characters can scarcely rise above the level of the tragi-comic. On the other hand, there is the more serious and sympathetic mind which is prepared to trace the outline of the human and the progressive beneath these commonplace people, and find there the essentials of tragedy.

In *Silas Marner*, finally, these problems of presentation are resolved by shifting the novel away from the verifiably and superficially realistic towards fable or folk-tale. For all George Eliot's success in giving Silas Marner a precise and historically specific social location, the reader need finally no more worry about his gentility or otherwise than he need worry about the gentility of Rumpelstiltskin. There is some comedy at the expense of the rustics in the Rainbow and their attempts at argument, but since we can read off in their clumsily formulated disagreements representative modern positions (on the limits of human knowledge, for example), this humour is readily subsumed in the greater pleasures of recognition. The interesting exception to this is Nancy Lammeter, who represents that thrifty and conscientious class, earlier championed in Mrs Poyser, who are indeed supposed to exist in the real world. For all her absence of education, we are told that she had 'the essential attributes of a lady' (*Silas Marner*, ch. 11); an assertion which again demonstrates, by its deference to notions of gentility, George Eliot's failure to be fully confident in those other notions of worth that she is elsewhere so keen to promote.

In all these early novels, then, George Eliot has to negotiate, in different ways and with different emphases, the various problems of claiming seriousness for her fictions. For that is what this oscillation between irony against the reader and irony against the characters finally indicates. These various problems, especially that of gentility, might seem external to the essential, human action; but in fact, as we have seen, it is precisely ways of seeing dominated by class that are likely to pose the biggest barrier to the novels being taken seriously at all. This is what George Eliot has to fight for, in those sections of the novels when she withdraws from the narrative to comment upon it—she is contending for an initial frame of reference in which recognition, solidarity and the flow of sympathy can occur.

II

We can now go on to consider more closely the ways in which the veraciously reported details of tenant-farming and provincial middle-class life can reveal the essential character-istics of human life fundamentally conceived. I have suggested that George Eliot finds it much harder to make this revelation in *The Mill on the Floss* than in the other early novels, and a comparison with *Adam Bede* will make the point more clearly. In the previous chapter we saw how *Adam Bede* could be described as a Feuerbachian novel, for in the character of Dinah Morris we had an especially clear example of how the essentially human qualities of affection and pity could be misunderstood as the workings of divinity but nevertheless transform and irradiate social life. This however is not the only way in which the divine operates in the world of Hayslope. The habits and manners of Adam Bede and the Poysers are equally important in contributing to the growing good of the world; there is a kind of workingday sacredness about the skill, thrift and dedication with which they go about their labour, in workshop, field, household and dairy. Adam says, for example:

> 'And God helps us with our headpieces and our hands as well as with our souls; and if a man does bits o' jobs out o' working hours—builds a oven for's wife to save her from going to the bake-house, or scrats at his bit o' garden and makes two potatoes grow instead o' one, he's doing more good, and he's just as near to God, as if he was running after some preacher and a-praying and a-groaning.' (*Adam Bede*, ch.1)

In saying this, he is saying no more than the truth, though of course we have to make the necessary inversion, so that we recognise that 'nearness to God' means nearness to the highest and most progressive faculties of humanity. Throughout the novel we are to recognise the supreme importance of doing a job well; for in a world ruled by the inexorable succession of consequences the one thing you can be certain of is the long-lasting benefit of labour honestly performed. Adam of course exemplifies this ethic—his ambition and enthusiasm run to building 'a bridge, or a town-hall, or a factory' (*Adam Bede*, ch. 33). But this ethic is

43

also to be found in the way that Mr Poyser runs the farm or the way that Mrs Poyser runs the farmhouse and the dairy. The delight and affection with which George Eliot dwells upon the details of Hayslope life, then, are to be explained not only by nostalgia for her childhood, or a Wordsworthian belief in the affective power of details around which associations have gathered; the delight and affection are equally the result of a confidence that in the details of this life, in the work ethic of this class, can be found a security for humanity's future.

Yet in *The Mill on the Floss* this confident synthesis of the affective and the practical has in effect broken down. The world of *Adam Bede* could be described as a positive organism, in which the habits and values of the dominant classes in the novel work beneficially in integrating the various members of society and in pushing forward the small and incremental changes which make up the process of evolution (though of course Hayslope signally fails to integrate Hetty Sorrel—but we are to understand this as her own fault, since she is a plant without roots, who has taken no nourishment from the potentially beneficent soil of Hayslope). In *The Mill on the Floss*, by contrast, society is still conceived organically, but it functions as a negative organism, where the habits and values of the Dodsons and Tullivers, the provincial middle class, operate as a powerful check on the development and growth of Maggie (and indeed Tom). Her own growth and moral selfhood are still produced in the myriad associations that gather round her past—' "If the past is not to bind us, where can duty lie?" ' (*Mill on the Floss*, VI, 14), she asks in her culminating rejection of Stephen. But this moral strength, supposedly rooted in the affective power of the past, in effect has no connection with the working and housekeeping rituals of the Dodsons and Tullivers, which have ossified into the forms of a religion dedicated to trivial ends.

Consider for example the occasion when the Tullivers visit the Pullets and are taken to see Aunt Pullet's new bonnet:

> So they went in procession along the bright and slippery corridor, dimly lighted by the semi-lunar top of the window, which rose above the closed shutter: it really was quite solemn. Aunt Pullet paused and unlocked a door which opened on something still more solemn than the passage—a darkened room, in which the outer light, entering feebly, showed what looked like the corpses of furniture in white shrouds. Everything that was not shrouded stood with its legs upwards. Lucy laid hold of Maggie's frock, and Maggie's heart beat rapidly. (*The Mill on the Floss*, I, 9)

This is no less than a parody of a religious service, with the eventual production of the bonnet producing the awe that belongs to the production of the Eucharist. But the very fact that it is a parody marks the distance of this novel from *Adam Bede*. In the earlier novel religion could be confidently assimilated to the processes of daily life with no sense either of irreverence or bathos. Here, however, Aunt Pullet's and Mrs Tulliver's sense of the sacred has become attached to the merely trivial and fashionable. Their level of religious culture is primitive—indeed it is strictly fetishistic in the Comtist sense[2]—and the whole scene permits knowing though perhaps affectionate laughter at the distance between this reverence and its trivial object. Throughout the novel the housekeeping habits of the Dodson sisters are the object of such laughter; their linen and their crockery have become the objects of fetish worship in a way that proves resistant to improvement.

This judgement needs qualification, of course. For one thing, George Eliot herself was horrified to learn that the novel was being read as an attack on the pettyness of English provincial life; though that does not make such a reading wrong, for in the novel she is setting in motion ideas and representations over which she cannot have complete control. More importantly, there is some countervailing effort within the novel to redeem the Dodson sisters. We learn, for example, that a 'sense of honour and rectitude . . . was a proud tradition in such families—a tradition which has been the salt of our provincial society' (*The Mill on the Floss*, I, 13). Perhaps more memorably, because supported by the narrative of the novel, Aunt Glegg is decisively redeemed when family loyalty leads her to stand by Maggie in her disgrace. Yet with this eccentric exception, the Dodsons and with them St Ogg's, remain stubbornly resistant to Maggie's real nobility.

It is for this reason that the very end of the novel becomes a series of recognitions. After her return to St Ogg's from the refused elopement with Stephen, Maggie is of course subjected to the ignorant obloquy of the town, and perhaps most importantly, she is rejected by Tom. The failure of St Ogg's and Tom to recognise the true scale of Maggie's moral worth is more than mere small-town narrow-mindedness: it represents exactly that absence of an 'outlet towards something beautiful, great or noble' about which George Eliot had earlier complained. It is thus very important, if the novel is to give any kind of hope for provincial life, that leading spirits of St Ogg's should be brought to recognise what Maggie has really done. Thus Dr Kenn, Bob Jakins, Philip Wakem and Lucy Deane are successively brought to an act of admiration. Finally, in the unreal world of the flood, the blinkers fall from Tom's eyes and he too recognises the truth. Yet the ending of the novel is deeply equivocal; for all the satisfactions these recognitions bring Maggie and the reader, it is very doubtful how far they actually contribute to the moral elevation of St Ogg's, of provincial life, itself.

We are now in a better position to see how the various notions, set out programmatically in that passage from 'The Natural History of German Life', work together in the novels; in particular, how the perception of fundamental human similarities and continuities (which founds the extension of sympathy) is linked to her notion of realism. You will recall how George Eliot rather flatly asserted in that passage that 'art is the nearest thing to life', suggesting that realism is an unproblematic term for her—it simply involves honestly reporting on what you see. However, we can now see that it involves a number of related notions which, when linked to the extension of sympathy, produce a powerful and confident aesthetic. (Later we shall want to ask whether this commonsense notion of realism is as tenable as it seems.) The related notions include an ethic of veracity and honesty in reporting; an attention to the this-worldly and the secular because attention to the other-worldly or unknowable is a useless distraction; and a refusal of the easy gratifications offered to the reader by idealising or picturesque art. The critic Raymond Williams gives a very useful brief discussion of the word 'realism' in his book *Keywords*, in which he describes how the term tended to imply, in the nineteenth century, both an insistence on veracious reporting ('photo-graphic realism') and a chastened refusal of the seductions of idealism or wish-fulfilment (as in 'let's be realistic').[3] George Eliot's early writing powerfully represents just this conjunction of understanding: as a writer she must report on the possibilities of the world as it is because it is the only world in which people can work out their salvation.

We saw in the discussion of *The Mill on the Floss*, however, that Geroge Eliot is by no means confident in all her writing that she *can* always trace the outlines of human progress in the details of ordinary life. Her realism is thus confident and even celebratory when she can make this alignment, when she is certain that the veraciously reported details of life signify the more fundamental, but equally 'real', relations of humanity. It is at its most anxious when it seems that the details of ordinary life refuse to form themselves into

47

meaningful patterns, when the induction to the general and fundamental truths is hard to make; for in such circumstances human life seems reduced to a mass of meaningless detail in which nothing is connected to anything else.

We can get some sense of the way George Eliot conceives of the relationship between the mundane and the fundamental (two aspects of the 'real') from the analogy she draws, in *Adam Bede*, with the way language signifies. She writes that:

> the finest language, I believe, is chiefly made up of unimposing words, such as *light, sound, stars, music*—words really not worth looking at, or hearing, in themselves, any more than *chips* or *sawdust*: it is only that they happen to be the signs of something unspeakably great and beautiful. I am of opinion that love is a great and beautiful thing too; and if you agree with me, the smallest signs of it will not be chips and sawdust to you; they will rather be like those little words, *light* and *music*, stirring the long-winding fibres of your memory, and enriching your present with your most precious past. (*Adam Bede*, ch. 50)

Words do no signify by virtue of any intrinsic capacity, but by virtue of the associations that they carry with them; these associations produce a powerful charge of emotion. In the same way, the small incidents of daily life do not themselves mean anything; they only do so if they point to the 'unspeakably great and beautiful' truths of which they are the signs. In one respect at least, however, the incidents of a novel do not resemble language as George Eliot describes it, for the writer cannot rely on the action of association to produce a powerful effect. Each novel is new—that's what 'novel' means, after all. Thus, to get the incidents of the novel to carry the full meanings she desires, George Eliot has first to ward off the potentially inappropriate associations deriving from other writing and its class-based expectations. She has also to insist on the significance of her stories and characters; in the absence of the kind of association that make words like 'light' and 'music' appear to speak for themselves, she must at once narrate and comment on her narration. She has both to provide reading for her readership and teach it how to read.

We can describe this relationship, in which the stories, characters and incidents stand in for or point to entities larger than themselves, as metonymic. Metonymy describes that kind of metaphor in which the part stands for the whole—the nineteenth century use of 'hands' for 'workers' (satirised by Dickens in *Hard Times*) is a peculiarly revealing example of metonymy. By extension we can use the term to describe the relationship of novel to world. The character of Mr Dempster in 'Janet's Repentance' signifies both the class of provincial lawyers and, more generally, the brutalised resistance of small-town provincial life to the higher influences of religion. Similarly, Adam Bede signifies both a class of self-improving and self-confident artisans and the better and more progressive elements of humanity in general. They are both metonyms of entities wider and greater than themselves.

It is worth discussing at greater length one kind of metonymy which is especially important in George Eliot's novels, because it reveals some interesting problems with the extension of sympathy. This is the relationship of part to whole usually described as typicality. We have noticed the insistence, in these early novels, on the ordinariness of the people and events that figure in the representations—a crucial stress if the extension of sympathy is to operate on appropriate objects. This sense of ordinariness requires that the characters are assumed to be typical in class or historical terms. Thus the Dodsons typify a whole section of English life, as indeed do the Poysers. The Poyser labourers are assumed to be typical farm-labourers. Even Silas Marner at the beginning of the novel is portrayed as a typical figure of the early nineteenth-century English landscape. The characters in the novel are to stand in for a whole class of people in the non-fictional world. Typicality of this kind amounts to statistical averaging; the reader's sympathies are claimed for such people just because they do represent the people with whom one comes in daily contact.

It is not usually the case, however, that typical characters of this kind can provide the heroes or heroines of the novels. The most important exception to this is Amos Barton, in whose mediocrity we see not only the average standard of the English clergy but the very average standard of ordinary human life.[4] He remains an exception, however; more usually we are to understand that the heroes and heroines of the novels transcend this kind of mundane or statistical typicality. We are specifically told that Adam Bede was 'not an average man' (*Adam Bede*, ch. 19); the stories of Mr Tryan, Dinah Morris, Maggie Tulliver or any of the heroes and heroines of the later novels would make no sense if we were not to understand their superiority to the mass of humanity that surrounds them. Indeed, we can recognise here a characteristic pattern in George Eliot's novels; they provide a hierarchy of ways of representing character, with the morally exceptional characters standing out against a background of socially typical humanity.

The heroes and heroines, however, are typical too—though in a way different from the statistical typicality of, say, Lawyer Wakem in *The Mill on the Floss*. They typify the fundamental human characteristics: it is above all in these central characters that the reader is to recognise the essentially human beneath or within the particularities of class or historical position. They provoke, in other words, a recognition of moral solidarity, while the socially typical characters that surround them provoke a recognition of social placing. It is above all the central characters of the novels who carry the humanly progressive or socially dynamic forces; it is in sympathising with *these* people that the reader's sympathies will be drawn out to the growing good of the world. Their typicality is that of the moral archetype, aligned with the specificities of class and historical position; the typicality of the characters who surround them is limited just to their place in the world.

There are thus two different kinds of typicality operating simultaneously in the novels, and the difference points to an important problem in the way George Eliot conceives of social change and human progress. For if we are to understand society organically, then the working-day habits and values of any society should jointly contribute to that society's growth and development. In fact, as we have seen, George Eliot is often anxious—and especially so in *The Mill on the Floss*—that she cannot trace such development in the ordinary fabric of English provincial life. She continually resorts to that superior moral power of exceptional people to provide the dynamic of social growth—a superior moral power which is difficult to explain in the precise social and historical terms sufficient for the ordinary fabric of life. This problem emerges as much in the method of representation, in the way the reader is to understand the typicality or otherwise of the characters, as it does in the logic of an argument. These formal characteristics of the novels, then, the various ways that they mean what they mean, are highly significant. Far from being a merely neutral vehicle for the significance of the novels, they themselves carry an ideological meaning.

III

I have described the project of the extension of our sympathies, with the accompanying notions of realism, as appearing to be directly egalitarian. One qualification we noted: the difficulty felt by George Eliot in extending the reader's sympathies to those classes whose habits and values seemed resistant to wider considerations—essentially working-class characters, whether rural or urban. We can now add a further qualification. The less characters appear as morally positive archetypes and the more they are to be understood as merely socially typcial, the greater the barrier they provide to a sympathy of moral solidarity. The very quality of the sympathy which the reader is asked to extend to the characters within the same novel can vary.

The first qualification to the apparent egalitarianism of the extension of sympathy is linked, we saw, to an ambivalence in George Eliot's understanding of 'the people'. This ambivalence is just as important in the vocabulary of mid-nineteenth-century politics, and, *mutatis mutandis*, in the political vocabulary of today. For 'the people' is a term which obscures as much as it designates. It has a genuine and poweful democratic appeal; but it can also elide differences between sections of 'the people' which are differences not only of wealth but of exploitation. We noticed how George Eliot herself, in defiance of her own prescriptions, could resort to the picturesque in writing about the Poysers' farm labourers. We could add that a similar kind of rose-tinted idealisation occurs with the character of Luke, the mill servant, in *The Mill on the Floss*, whose loyalty to his employer would have been pleasantly consolatory to the middle-class readers of the novel. Both those kinds of idealisation—and others like them—work towards keeping that split obscure, a split best understood as one between employers and their employed. A difficulty or inconsistency in the artistic achievements managed by George Eliot in her novels is thus cognate with a split in the vocabulary of popular politics. It is not that politics cause the artistic difficulties; rather a comparable class-position in politics and art produces comparable difficulties, though worked out in the forms and conventions appropriate to each separate area.

A more radical qualification to the egalitarianism of the 'extension of our sympathies' now requires to be made, however. For perhaps sympathy is a less straightforwardly positive emotion than George Eliot assumes. It is not just its nearness to pity that is a problem, though Blake's objection to pity remains as powerful as ever:

> Pity would be no more
> If we did not make somebody poor.[5]

More particularly, we can ask whether the very claims made for sympathy by George Eliot do not create as many difficulties as they seek to resolve. Sympathy, we saw, was to strengthen social cohesion, to bind people together in a social organism threatened by the exclusiveness of class. Class, however, is more than a question of consciousness; the stultifying and destructive effects of class are not confined to snobbishness. More fundamentally class is a material distinction, determining different positions and rewards in the labour process. The attempt to bind people together in society, to gain recognition for people on the strength of their moral rather than their social worth, obscures these real material differences that will continue to divide people no matter with what sympathy 'we' regard our 'more heavily-laden fellow-men'.

This is especially the case given the kind of realism that characterises George Eliot's writing—the sympathetic look that pierces the distracting differences of class or historical position to recognise the essentially human that exists beneath these material accidents. Insight of this kind is comforting to the reader, even self-confirming. It might disturb his or her comfortable assumptions about class, and the worth of people in other classes; but in the act of recognition, in the act of seeing 'someone like me' beneath

53

those 'superficial' class differences, their fundamental, material importance can be cancelled.

One final qualification needs to be made, which is connected to this question of the novels' readership. The fact is that George Eliot's novels presuppose at least two different readerships: a naive and a sophisticated one. The bracing of social ties which is the object of the extension of sympathies is common to both; it acts almost by stealth. But the directly intellectual understanding of her narratives, for which she resorts to Feuerbach, or Comte, or other thinkers whose work she has assimilated, is only available to a sophisticated and knowledgeable readership. In one sense it is a *tour de force* that she can make the language of Evangelicalism, or the speech rhythms of Midlands artisans, or the primitive religious ideas of Nancy Lammeter in *Silas Marner*, sound like the advanced intellectual positions to which she subscribes. However, a contemporary reader's ability to 'translate' such language in the appropriate way is directly related to his or her class and educational position, and George Eliot is quite content if the uneducated reader's naive religious convictions are reinforced rather than undermined, for the naive understanding of Mr Tryan's or Adam Bede's ideas is just as socially bracing. The Christian reader could certainly read *Adam Bede* without realising that it is not a Christian book. George Eliot was most anxious that her novels should appeal to the 'élite', but equally desired, and rightly, that her novels should be popular. At times this dual ambition produces a kind of equivocation in her writing, so that it can be read simultaneously in two different ways. This equivocation is unavoidably élitist.

I have made these three qualifications to the project of the extension of our sympathies in an effort to suggest that that project is a less straightforwardly positive one than might at first appear. These qualifications might seem excessively hostile to George Eliot. They do nevertheless suggest how her own class and historical position set limits to her artistic project. It is this position, and the intellectual problems associated with it, that lead her to make her characteristic humanist move in piercing through the surface of the historically specific to the humanly general. If we can see the historical determinants of that we are better placed to resist the too easy assimilation of George Eliot's writing, over a century after her death, to a critical view which, for its own contemporary purposes, wishes to assert that humanity in its essentials transcends history. We shall discuss more closely how she conceives history in the following chapter, taking *Romola* and *Felix Holt* as our principal texts.

3

'The Growing Good of the World'

I

All of George Eliot's novels, with the exception of *Daniel Deronda*, are novels of the past, set in a period at least a generation before their time of writing. The reasons for this are multiple; but one result is that all the novels implicitly pose questions of historical change and advance. It is to such questions that this chapter is addressed, especially in relation to *Romola* and *Felix Holt, the Radical*; but the discussion is equally relevant to the other novels—indeed, it is from the 'Finale' to *Middlemarch* that I take the title of this chapter.

Romola, however, differs substantially from all of George Eliot's other novels. It is set very much further in the past, and it is her only foreign novel. It should be said, also, that it has proved least popular and least successful. In many ways *Romola* marks a transition in George Eliot's career. She famously remarked: 'I began it a young woman—I finished it an old woman.' She forsook her old publisher, John Blackwood, to publish the novel in the *Cornhill Magazine*, a prestigious form of publication and also a very lucrative one. She wrote *Romola* as a successful novelist, diffident about her own powers as ever, of course, but nevertheless able to rely on her own success as an entry into her readers' confidence. And she consciously directed the book at a more élite readership, writing to Sara Hennell that 'of necessity, the book is addressed to fewer readers than my previous works, and I myself have never expected—I might rather say intended—that the book should be as "popular" in the same sense as the others.'[1]

Romola represents an important break from the earlier novels in other respects as well, however. Together with *Felix Holt* (and indeed the poem *The Spanish Gypsy*, published in 1868), it shows evidence of a considerable re-ordering of her aesthetic priorities. Briefly, the synthesis represented by the 'extension of sympathy', of an aesthetic of realism linked to a faith in human progress, has broken down in George Eliot's writings of the 1860s. We saw the fragility of that synthesis in *The Mill on the Floss*; in *Romola* and *Felix Holt* the synthesis is irrevocably broken, with fundamental consequences for George Eliot's writing.

The breakdown in that synthesis, and the way that George Eliot conceives of historical change, are intimately connected. I shall approach this topic by way of two main questions: What is the main agency of social change? And, what is implied in writing novels about the past? Some suggested answers to these questions form the substance of this chapter. However, the breakdown and reconstruction of George Eliot's aesthetic does not only represent a re-ordering of her own, personal intellectual and artistic thinking; it is symptomatic of a wider crisis in liberal thought in the 1860s. Not only George Eliot, but Matthew Arnold and even the greatest liberal thinker of the nineteenth century, John Stuart Mill, adopted positions in that decade which provide serious qualifications to the confident progressivism of earlier liberalism. The 1860s, after all, was the decade of the second Reform crisis, when an increasingly confident working class demanded the extension of the franchise. It cannot be too highly emphasised that *Felix Holt* (and indeed *Middlemarch*) looks back on the earlier Reform crisis of the 1830s from the perspective of the later one. In the face of working-class demands for an extension of the franchise, George Eliot, Arnold and Mill all resorted to alternatives which would privilege the operation of knowledge in the working of the social system. For Arnold this meant the emphasis on 'culture' in *Culture and Anarchy* (1867), understood to mean an area of historically sifted and therefore reliable knowledge which could be brought to bear upon the disputes of the present. Mill, though he remained fundamentally committed to the extension of the franchise, nevertheless felt compelled to suggest a complex system of proportional representation to ensure a proper influence for the highly educated (in *Representative Government* (1861)), and deeply distrusted the ballot. George Eliot herself was fundamentally antipathetic to politics—in the narrow sense anyway. Her distrust was given covert but forceful expression in essays such as 'Servants' Logic', which under the cover of amusement at the foibles of cooks, suggests that 'a mild yet firm authority' rather than misguided attempts at explanation is the only way to guarantee good domestic service—with the explicit consequence that servants and others of their class are so resistant to rational explanation of the causes of things that to give them the franchise is the wildest folly.[2]

This is George Eliot writing at her least generous and least sympathetic. Nevertheless, both *Romola* and *Felix Holt* are fundamentally marked by this broken confidence in the onwardness of collective life. The ordinary, everyday habits and beliefs of the majority of people can hold no hope for growth and development, which is to be understood almost exclusively as being produced by the higher moral and affective capacities of exceptional individuals. These novels thus provide in more extreme form further evidence of that split, in methods of characterisation and in ways of conceiving historical change, that we noticed in the earlier novels.

This is not to say, of course, that the extension of sympathy—the habitual reflex of George Eliot's writing—is not informing her representations of everyday Florentine life in *Romola*, or of provincial English life in the early 1830s in *Felix Holt*. Indeed, the earlier novel, set in late fifteenth-century Italy, explicitly tackles the problem of finding the commonly human beneath the apparently strange and foreign. And, as we noticed in the earlier novels, this characteristic aesthetic strategy is accompanied by a sense of competing representations present in contemporary writing. The representation of Catholicism in *Romola* provides a typical example. Catholics were still objects of intense prejudice in the mid-nineteenth century, and contemporary novels, especially the vast numbers of religious ones, are full of hostile representations of Catholics. George Eliot, however, is prepared to describe in minute and sympathetic detail an intensely Catholic religious procession, and finds ways of defending it which stress its value despite the alien and disturbingly unprotestant symbols: '"the great bond of our Republic is expressing itself in ancient symbols, without which the vulgar would be conscious of nothing beyond their own petty wants of back and stomach, and never rise to the sense of community in religion and law. There has been no great people without processions"' (*Romola*, ch. 8). This forceful defence of processions, typically assimilating even an alien religion as a socially cohesive agency, is just one instance of the extension of sympathy across barriers of religious and historical distance. In a similar but more familiar way the characterisation of the Independent Minister, Rufus Lyon, in *Felix Holt* actively challenges the genteel reader to recognise

59

his real nobility and 'moral elevation' despite the unfashionableness of his religious denomination. The reader is to recognise this, indeed, even when the limited perspectives of the inhabitants of Treby Magna prevent them from doing so: 'Perhaps it required a larger power of comparison than was possessed by any of that audience to appreciate the moral elevation of an Independent minister who could utter these words' (*Felix Holt*, ch. 46). As in the early novels, the mind that has 'a large vision of relations' (the narrator's) can enable the reader to appreciate nobility in unexpected places, and thus bolster the ties of sympathy in society at large.

However, despite this habitual attempt to find the basis of sympathy in apparently alien conditions, there remains some point to the criticism that has repeatedly been made of *Romola*, that the extraordinarily minute and detailed account of everyday Florentine life actually functions as a distraction. George Eliot is on the horns of a dilemma. If, as she believes, the real meaning of human lives is in part to be found in everyday habits and manners, then she is obliged to give a great deal of attention to providing full and accurate information in such matters as fifteenth century Florentine dress, speech, amusements, day-to-day politics, architecture, and so on. However, the more she does this the more she runs the risk of alienating her contemporary reader, who is likely to find the accumulation of such detail a barrier to the extension of sympathy. In recognising this as a dilemma we do not have to defer to those criticisms of the novel which stress its laboriousness, or that 'it smells of the lamp'—criticisms which imply unwarranted post-Romantic assumptions about art being spontaneous and unlearnt (the first to make such a criticism was G.H. Lewes himself, who wrote to John Blackwood to get him to 'discountenance the idea of a Romance being the product of an Encyclopedia'.)[3] Rather, we can see *Romola* as posing in particularly acute form a problem which confronts many realist novels—the problem of ensuring that the provision of detail, necessary to provide the effect in the reader of being present at simple, ordinary life, can always be interpreted in the appropriate ways to give sense to the wider continuities of the novel—of character, significant milieu, theme or doctrine. In fact, there is no way of ensuring this appropriate interpretation—metonymy is perhaps inherently unstable. *Romola* repeatedly stalls in this attempted movement from detail to significance; the cumulative effect of so much unfamiliar detail, which has constantly to be glossed, explained or translated, is to render the city of Florence not only strange but rather dull.

These barriers to the consciousness of human solidarity are created by the very fact of writing a historical novel set in a distant time and place. There are, however, other difficulties which *Romola* shares with the more familiar English setting of *Felix Holt*. In both novels the actual habits and values of popular life tend to obscure or discount the wider values to which the nobler characters, and through them George Eliot, are committed. We can see this most clearly in relation to the defeat of Savonarola, the central historical character of the novel, who wakens Romola to submission and religious duty. Indeed, the very fact of describing his history as a martyrdom sets up an opposition between individual heroism and popular stupidity. Moreover, the active agents of his defeat, men like Tito Melema and Dolfo Spini, provide a constantly cynical and belittling perspective with which they are capable of effectively intervening in the body politic. Tito's cynical view that the sentiment of society is 'a mere tangle of anomalous traditions and opinions' (*Romola*, ch. 11), nevertheless enables him to get the ear of society, much as Dolfo Spini is capable of acting on men's baser passions to effect Savonarola's defeat. Public collective life, in fact, is especially likely to be the arena of small-minded and selfish motives. The only counterpoise to this is Romola's own eventual sanctity, her own acknowledgement of and submission to the higher duties of affection and altruism. Though we are to understand this as in itself a social if not a narrowly political value, this separation of the political and the personal bespeaks a narrowed confidence in the possibilities of collectively induced progress.

Similar but much more acutely pressing problems beset *Felix Holt*. The novel is in part concerned with the ability to see beyond the narrow possibilities and interests of English provincial life in the early 1830s, precisely because that life is so pre-eminently not the home of anything higher or nobler. The inhabitants of the town of Treby Magna do not even have the eccentric interest of the Dodsons in *The Mill on the Floss*; their conversation is uniformly ignorant and misinformed. The exceptions to this are Rufus Lyon and Felix Holt himself. Rufus Lyon's 'moral elevation', we noticed, is likely to remain unremarked by his fellow townsmen; indeed, it is a source of constant anxiety to him that the wider perspectives with which he views the apparently small events of Treby remain dim or unseen to other people. ' "We are left to judge by uncertain signs" ' (*Felix Holt*, ch. 37), he remarks; and the the novel is in part concerned with this uncertainty. It even affects the narrator, who at one point feels obliged to forestall the possibility of the Rev. Lyon appearing merely laughable:

> but I never smiled at Mr Lyon's trustful energy without falling to penitence and veneration immediately after. For what we call illusions are often, in truth, a wider vision of past and present realities—a willing movement of a man's soul with the larger sweep of the world's forces—a movement towards a more assured end than the chances of a single life. (*Felix Holt*, ch. 16)

This anxiety haunts the book: that the wider, truer or larger forces which give dignity and nobility even to these small lives will remain unseen, or be discounted as illusory.

Esther Lyon's conversion, in the course of the novel, is thus a conversion which brings her to acknowledge the existence of motives and realities beyond the trivial concerns with which she is preoccupied at the beginning of the story. Early on we are told that 'her life was a heap of fragments, and so were her thoughts; some great energy was needed to bind them together' (*Felix Holt*, ch. 15); that energy is provided by Felix Holt. Yet the constant pressure of provincial life is predominantly in the opposite direction—towards the enforcement of trivial ambitions of a socially self-seeking kind. While Rufus Lyon, not without a touch of irony, can enjoy 'that serenity and elevation of mind which is infallibly brought by a preoccupation with the wider relations of things' (*Felix Holt*, ch. 15), the more characteristic attitude in Treby Magna is that of Mr Christian, who 'had that sort of cleverness which is said to "know the world"—that is to say, he knew the price-current of most things' (*Felix Holt*, ch. 36). A number of scenes in the novel demonstrate how ordinary lives are lived at the level of the most sordid and petty ignorance. Chapter 7, for example, largely set in the steward's room of the local Manor, concerns a discussion of the Reform Bill amongst the servants and their friends. Their conversation and their merrymaking is subject to the most unpleasant and ungenerous contempt. Similarly, the conversation of the town's shopkeepers, and of the thoroughly unenlightened local miners, all testify to the predominant stupidity and triviality of Treby life.

We have come a long way in *Felix Holt*, then, from the happy confidence in the 'working-day world' which characterised *Adam Bede*. Comparable if less developed difficulties beset *The Mill on the Floss* we saw; and as in the earlier novel, there is an important recognition scene at the end of this novel also, when the true nobility both of Rufus Lyon and Felix Holt (falsely accused of leading a riot) is established—to the reader's satisfaction anyway. This diminished confidence in the possibilities of popular life, however, produces a compensatory shift in the characterisation of the heroes and heroines; Romola and Felix Holt are much more frankly idealistic in ways which would have been out of place in the earlier novels.

For the broken confidence in the ability of ordinary life to generate social change or improvement is necessarily accompanied by a resort to idealising characterisation, essential if any faith in the onwardness of life is to be maintained. It is in this way that the earlier synthesis, of realism with sympathy, has been broken down and reconstituted. In the earlier novels some guarantees for the future could be found in the ordinary lives of ordinary people. In *Romola* and *Felix Holt* this is no longer the case. The ordinary lives of ordinary people tend to act as a drag on the nobler aspirations of exceptional individuals.

Of course, this is a pattern that is already potentially present in the earlier books—the Rev. Tryan, Dinah Morris and Maggie Tulliver, we noted, already have the typicality of moral archetypes. However, unlike Romola or Felix Holt, the Rev. Tryan and Dinah Morris at least belonged to historically real religious movements—Evangelicalism and Methodism—which, however we might want to judge them now, provide possible explanations, situated in the real world, of how these people might come to be what they are. In a different but comparable way, the exceptional history of Maggie Tulliver does credibly emerge from the carefully established milieu of the mill on the Floss. By contrast, there is little attempt made to suggest where either Romola's or Felix Holt's exceptional capacities might have come from. Certainly, Savonarola's influence on Romola is decisive, but in the end she transcends it to become, in a deliberately symbolic portion of the book, a representative of the very highest capacities of humanity itself, precisely conceived ahistorically. The case of Felix Holt is if anything still more striking. Though he is called a Radical in the book's subtitle (and indeed calls himself one), his Radicalism is of a kind that was never seen in heaven or earth. It is a specifically anti-political kind of Radicalism, which is attached to no real historical movement whatsoever. The only explanation we are given of how Felix came to believe and act in the way that he does is that it was as a result of revulsion at a bout of (wholly unspecified) debauchery. It is in this sense that Romola and Felix Holt are idealised: their presence cannot be explained by the careful circumstantial accounting which is adequate for other characters in the novels.

Let us be clear that this idealism on George Eliot's part is not a failure of her realism, but an aesthetic strategy produced by her perception of realism's inadequacy. I have suggested that one of the main anxieties of *Felix Holt* especially is that life should be no more than what it seems to the trivialising perspectives of provincial England. This fear, produced by a diminished confidence in ordinary life, accompanies a diminished confidence in a realism understood as a form of writing tied to the actually existent. The other side of the same coin is a socially and historically unlocated idealisation of character. Take both these tendencies together and you have a double movement which seeks to resolve a fundamental contradiction in George Eliot's notion of historical progress.

This re-ordered synthesis now demands a reliance on idealised characterisation earlier in George Eliot's career dismissed as a distraction. Idealism of character—of those characters who, like Romola and Felix Holt, and of course Dorothea Brooke in *Middlemarch*, are to carry forward the highest qualities of humanity, but in ways which are unpolitical, reliable and 'incalculably diffusive'—such idealisation points to a notion of historical change rather different from the inclusive organicism to which George Eliot was committed in *Adam Bede* and, less confidently, in *The Mill on the Floss*. In fact, it is rather nearer to a very conventional notion of change, in which the heroic individual, independently of, or even in spite of, his surrounding society (understood as 'circumstances'), carries things forward. The implications of the novels are rather different from this, because character and social milieu are still felt to be mutually reactive. Nevertheless, both *Romola* and *Felix Holt* give the impression that it is character that reacts upon social milieu in a positive way, while the milieu reacts only adversely upon character.

This is still a kind of organicism. George Eliot defended her accumulation of detail in *Romola* by saying: 'It is the habit of my imagination to strive after as full a vision of the medium in which a character moves as of the character itself';[4] and 'medium' here recalls the fluid in which an organism lives, such as the sea-water in which G.H. Lewes studies his animalcules for physiological purposes. In this version of organicism individual organisms are conceived as separate centres of energy. George Eliot writes of 'that mixture of pushing forward and being pushed forward, which is a brief history of most human things' (*Felix Holt*, ch. 33). Many of her formulations of determination are cognate with this assertion. However, the implications of the organic analogy here are very different from the implications of the analogy if the whole of society is conceived as a single organism rather than the 'medium' for lots of organisms. In this latter case progress and historical change are more likely to be seen as resulting from cumulative, collective effort.

The organic analogy, then, has different and even contradictory implications. A related metaphor, that of the web, is equally unstable, and in precisely comparable ways. The metaphor is most famously used in *Middlemarch*, when George Eliot uses it to suggest the totality of human lives that make up provincial society: 'I at least have so much to do in unravelling certain human lots, and seeing how they were woven and interwoven, that all the light I can command must be concentrated on this particular web' (*Middlemarch*, ch. 15). The metaphor is present, however, not only in various more or less explicit ways elsewhere in *Middlemarch*, but also in the other novels—as, for instance, in Tito's use of 'tangle' to describe the traditions and opinions that make up the sentiment of society. In short, it is a powerful and multiply suggestive metaphor for the social totality. Yet its very suggestiveness makes for an instability so radical as to enable the metaphor to mean quite contradictory things. If society resembles a web, are we to think of the people who make it up as being the filaments of the web, or as being somehow caught in it? Certainly in the sentence I have just quoted from *Middlemarch* the former sense is dominant—the web is used to give a sense of the actions and interactions of various people who themselves make up its warp and its woof. Yet if we think of the actual histories of Lydgate and Dorothea, we are much more likely to think of the web as a net in which they are caught, as in the following description of Lydgate 'feeling the hampering threadlike pressure of small social conditions, and their frustrating complexity' (*Middlemarch*, ch. 18). In this instance Lydgate has become a Gulliver trapped by myriad Lillliputtion threads. He is not part of the web precisely because it is holding him down.

This unstable suggestiveness of the metaphor of the web is analogous, then, with the different implications of the different kinds of organicism present in *Romola* and *Felix Holt*. The way one conceives of historical change can differ enormously depending on how the stress is laid, and in the two novels we are most concerned with here, that stress tends to fall most upon the character in its medium. If this tells of a diminished confidence in the possibilities of popular life, now solely a beneficiary of individual nobility, it yet produces its own difficulties. Consider, for example, the endings of both *Romola* and *Felix Holt*. In the earlier novel general disgust with Florentine life leads Romola to leave her native city. She returns after ministering to a plague-stricken village (to the villagers she seems like the Virgin Mary, whom she resembles in a Feuerbachian way), and leads a little matriarchal community to which representative Florentine citizens are suitably deferential. The problem with this sequence is not that it is symbolic but rather what it symbolises—a form of life dedicated to the higher duties of memory (to Savonarola's legacy) and affection (of parent and child), but quite cut off from the popular life of the city. As for Felix, he leaves Treby Magna altogether, engaged in another town on some quite unspecified project of social reform: '"Where great things can't happen, I care for very small things, such as will never be known beyond a few garrets and workshops"' (*Felix Holt*, ch. 45). It is a position which certainly has its own logic, but quite apart from the enormously reduced notion of Radicalism it implies, it is a resolution quite unrelated to the life and problems of Treby Magna as we have seen them in the novel.

Romola and *Felix Holt*, then, both have great difficulty in imagining how the nobler or higher capacities of those to whom George Eliot is most committed, will actually work to the benefit of social life. The popular life of both Florence and Treby Magna is itself conceived in ways which make it resistant to the transforming influence of those with wider perspectives. In *Felix Holt* in particular, George Eliot finds it very hard to sympathise with substantial sections of English society; she demonstrates a pessimism about the capacities of collective life to regenerate itself which produces in turn an idealised and socially unlocated conception of individual character as the source of social improvement. This pessimism will be a dominant feature of *Middlemarch*.

II

However George Eliot concevies of historical change, and whatever its effective agents, it is clear that the processes of social improvement are slow and even minutely accumulative. Social dynamics (to use the phraseology of both Comte and Spencer) needs always to be conceived in the context of social statics, the study of those fundamentals of human life which in their view remained unchanging across the ages, and put absolute limits to the possibilities of human variation. The representation of late fifteenth-century Florence is certainly conceived in this spirit, to the extent that we may wish to ask whether *Romola* can be called an historical novel at all. The opening paragraph of the 'Proem' to the novel gives striking expression to the notion of social statics:

> The great river-courses which have shaped the lives of men have hardly changed; and those other streams, the life-currents that ebb and flow in human hearts, pulsate to the same great needs, the same great loves and terrors. As our thought follows close in the slow wake of the dawn, we are impresed with the broad sameness of the human lot, which never alters in the main headings of its history—hunger and labour, seed-time and harvest, love and death. (*Romola*, 'Proem')

Though we have seen that when she descends to the particularities of Florentine life, George Eliot actually finds it very difficult to impress the 'broad sameness of the human lot', at this level of generality this assertion carries more power. What rescues the paragraph from a merely conventional cancelling of history is its insistence upon the material constraints that limit human life; the whole passage is far from consolatory, especially not the legitimately solemn and conclusive cadence of the final phrase. The passage represents a typical example of one element of George Eliot's aesthetic, linked to her rejection of the consolations of religion: to insist upon the hard and unchangeable conditions of human life, above all the unavoidable fact of death, will perhaps teach us to be kinder to each other in the time we have available. It is another way of enforcing sympathy, though now sanctioned by the highest possible perspective.

One answer to our second question, then—what are the implications of writing novels about the past?—is that at a sufficient level of generality, it makes no fundamental difference. Not only here, but throughout her novels, George Eliot insists that the unchanging conditions of humanity ensure fundamental continuities of experience across the passage of time. When she writes, in *Felix Holt*, that 'the harder problems of our life have changed less than our manners; we wrestle with the old sorrows, but more decorously' (*Felix Holt*, ch. 40), the style may be less elevated but the implications are the same as the passage from *Romola*. What history has to teach us, if we have the insight to learn it, is the relative unimportance of historical change.

For all George Eliot's eloquence in the passage from the 'Proem', the whole position is nevertheless open to some serious objections. The same great conditions of human life—of material need, sexuality and mortality—indeed persist across the ages, for these are the very conditions of our biological being. But the ways that they have been understood, felt or acted upon have obviously varied so radically and dramatically that we cannot simply rely on the presence of these constraints to ensure similarity of experience. Factors other than biology, such as the level of technology, the division of labour, the respective positions of men and women, are fundamental in forming the ways we understand, and thus experience, those biological constants; these factors are pre-eminently subject to historical change. The interaction of social statics and social dynamics is doubtless more complicated than George Eliot, and the intellectual tradition of which she is a part, assumes.

This perhaps rather general objection becomes more directly pertinent when we consider the kind of continuity of experience upon which George Eliot insists in *Romola*. Perhaps the best example is the whole narrative of Tito Melema, the superficially attractive but basically selfish Greek who marries Romola only to trample on the dearest affections and memories of her life. The novel minutely dissects how his pleasure-loving nature, and his refusal to act upon his deeper obligations, gradually and inexorably entail a succession of consequences that work to his destruction. The story is thus an extensive object lesson in the application of the law of consequences to morality: the results of selfish actions, like the results of all actions, are both wide-spreading and inevitable. This of course is a thoroughly nineteenth-century idea, though this by no means disqualifies its relevance to the fifteenth century: the law of gravity may have been discovered by Newton but that doesn't mean that people before him could stand on the ceiling! The problem occurs with the extent of Tito's understanding of the law of consequences, the extent, in other words, of the correspondence between his subjective self-understanding and our modern understanding of him.

Consider, for example, the following comment, provoked by Tito's readiness to contemplate multiple treachery in the complex politics of Florence:

> Our lives make a moral tradition for our individual selves, as the life of mankind at large makes a moral tradition for the race; and to have once acted nobly seems a reason why we should always be noble. But Tito was feeling the effect of an opposite tradition: he had won no memories of self-conquest and perfect faithfulness from which he could have a sense of falling. (*Romola*, ch. 39)

The comment enforces the continuity of experience between

71

then and now, and between the characters in the novel and the reader, an effect won, of course, by the inclusive use of 'our' and 'we'. However, the passage is not far from anachronism, from the unwarrantable assumption that late Florentine understanding of life and morality is identical with the understanding of the nineteenth century. For the generalising and inclusive comment which introduces the passage is an extension of the law of consequences; it expresses a cherished Positivist idea that the history of an individual must recapitulate the history of humanity, with everybody learning in their own lives to make the passage from egoism to altruism, just as humanity at large must do so. This difficulty arises not because George Eliot uses this idea; it is not only legitimate but even desirable that she should make explicit the kind of judgement she is using to make sense of and to place Tito and the other people of fifteenth-century Florence. The difficulty of anachronism arises because it is in the interest of her humanism to obscure the difference between her contemporary understanding and that of the Florentines. Thus it seems ultimately unclear exactly what Tito was feeling—to say he was 'feeling the effect of an opposite tradition' (anyway only defined negatively) leaves unclear the extent to which he understands the cause of the effect. If he were to do so the writing would become evidently anachronistic; but if he has no sense of it the humanist translation of one culture into another would become impossible.

The case of Tito is suggestive, then, of the difficulties which beset the attempt to assimilate the past to the categories and understanding of the present; we shall discuss the gap between the understandings of characters and narrator more fully in the following chapter on *Middlemarch*. It is not only at this grand level of social statics, however, that George Eliot seeks to assert the continuity of experience between past and present. In both *Romola* and *Felix Holt* she uses the past to illuminate the present by tracing analogies and similarities of a more direct and particular kind. In the remainder of this chapter we shall consider some of these analogies and their implications; they provide further indications of the way history is presented in the novels.

If it is the case that a more general crisis in liberalism in the 1860s covertly determines the re-ordering of her aesthetic strategies, it is also the case that she uses her novels of this time explicitly to discuss some of the features of that crisis. In *Romola*, George Eliot can find sufficient grounds to draw an analogy between late fifteenth-century Florence and nineteenth-century England on the general question of the relationship between secular knowledge and religion. In *Felix Holt*, it is above all the questions of the franchise, and of the place of politics in social life—both acute problems in the 1860s—that are discussed in the context of the earlier Reform crisis of the 1830s; but George Eliot uses this as an opportunity for a wide-ranging assessment of the achievements of the bourgeois transformation of English political life heralded by the first Reform Act of 1832.

The question of the franchise is a live one in Florence as well, though it is a subsidiary issue to the main themes of the book. Much more important is the way the novel broaches some of the central intellectual issues of the mid-nineteenth century; indeed they might be said to be its *raison d'être*. We have seen that much of the intellectual energy of George Eliot's career was directed to finding a wider and more inclusive set of beliefs that would retain the social efficacy of religion while discarding the outmoded doctrinal content. She uses the intellectual positions of Renaissance Italy to work through this problem, pitting the new knowledge of the rediscovery of the classics against the religious energy and enthusiasm of Savonarola and his followers. The career of Romola, which we have already seen working out the logic of the split between the popular and the personal, also enacts

73

the transition from a barren intellectualism, through religious enthusiasm, to a position in which her own human capacities of affection and submission to duty can act in socially binding ways, without the external authority of an other-worldly sanction. The novel has rightly been called a 'Positivist allegory'.[5] What this implies, however, is George Eliot's skill (as I earlier suggested, perhaps a misplaced ingenuity) in finding multiple parallels and comparisons between her own time and the Italian Renaissance.

Unsurprisingly, the analogy between the England of the early 1830s, represented in *Felix Holt*, and the England of the 1860s, is much more direct and immediate. The novel, in fact, is a tract for the times, directly addressed to central questions of the 1860s. What does real social improvement mean? Can it be achieved through parliamentary reform? Is the arena of parliamentary politics so corrupt that nothing can be done there without corrupting oneself? Would the ballot rather than a public show of hands, eliminate corruption? How are we to assess the changes in English life that have occurred between the 1830s and the 1860s? It is to these questions that the book is addressed, and as such it stands as a judgement on the whole programme of the liberal middle-class transformation of English society that occurred during the first half of the nineteenth century.

You can best get a sense of the way this transformation appears in the novel from the justly famous 'Introduction' that George Eliot provides. Unfortunately, it is too long to quote in full here; but the beginning of the second paragraph makes the issues clear:

> In those days there were pocket boroughs, a Birmingham unrepresented in parliament and compelled to make strong representations out of it, unrepealed corn laws, three-and-sixpenny letters, a brawny and many-breeding pauperism, and other departed evils; but there were some pleasant things too, which have also departed. (*Felix Holt*, 'Introduction')

The list of 'departed evils' precisely represents the main targets of the bourgeois reforms accomplished since 1830: undue aristocratic influence on Parliament ('pocket-boroughs'); an unfair and irrational system of representation which took no account of new industrial centres; protection for the landed interest against the free operation of the market ('unrepealed corn laws'); an unreformed postal service, since transformed by Rowland Hill's penny post; and an uneconomic system of poor relief which encouraged able-bodied pauperdom and the 'breeding' of pauper children—a system abolished by the Poor Law of 1834. Against this list of undoubted improvements, George Eliot sets the pleasures of a stage-coach ride—since superseded, of course, by the railway. Chief amongst such pleasures is the delight of the hedgerows, described in rich and particular detail:

> It was worth the journey only to see those hedgerows, the liberal homes of unmarketable beauty—of the purple-blossomed, ruby-berried nightshade, of the wild convulvulus climbing and spreading in tendrilled strength till it made a great curtain of pale-green hearts and white trumpets, of the many-tubed honeysuckle which, in its most delicate fragrance, hid a charm more subtle and penetrating than beauty. (*Felix Holt*, 'Introduction')

The point about this beauty is that it is 'unmarketable', that it represents a value in life outside of the purely rational and purposeful operations of the market. In this respect, even the way that the hedgerow flowers are described is part of a significant contrast—the accumulation of adjectives, the wildly-spreading tendrils, all point to qualities irreducible to modern rule and method. The landscape through which the stage-coach travels, then, is one which is understood in terms of a contrast between contemporary reformed rationality and a past ignorant, unreformed, but nevertheless charged with value.

This is not far from nostalgia, though George Eliot is careful to insist, in the remainder of the paragraph, that for all the claims made for it, this English countryside was nevertheless the home of ignorance and dirt. The movement of the whole passage, then, is undoubtedly to endorse the programme of progress and reform, but also to suggest what it excludes: those elements of life, like the hedgerows, which gather value even though they are 'unmarketable'. In one sense this is the conservatism of middle age—George Eliot was nearly fifty when she wrote this passage, and can surely be allowed some nostalgia for the landscape of her childhood. But in other, less purely personal senses, this unresolvable opposition between valued past and rational present is doubly suggestive. It is symptomatic of George Eliot's difficulty in reconciling a system of value based upon memory, association and the affections, with a commitment to rational and progressive improvement. It is also symptomatic of the sense of loss created when market relations replace customary and traditional relations, when things are no longer valued for their use but are only valued for what they will fetch—their 'price-current', to use a phrase of Mr Christian's in the novel.

The transformation of Treby itself is certainly to be understood as being brought about by its integration into the national market. The Treby of 1830 is in the process of change, and George Eliot insists on the importance of understanding this process:

> Such was the old-fashioned, grazing, brewing, wool-packing, cheese-loading life of Treby Magna, until there befell new conditions, complicating its relating with the rest of the world, and gradually awakening in it that higher consciousness which is known to bring higher pains. (*Felix Holt*, ch. 3)

And:

In this way it happened that Treby Magna gradually passed from being simply a respectable market-town—the heart of a great rural district, where the trade was only such as had close relations with the local landed interest—and took on the more complex life brought by mines and manufactures, which belong more directly to the great circulating system of the nation that to the local systems to which they have been superadded. (*Felix Holt*, ch. 3)

Treby Magna, in fact, is undergoing what we have come to call the Industrial Revolution; but George Eliot can understand this as a form of Spencerian evolution: the social life of Treby is passing from one stage of complexity, characterised by local market relations, to the higher level of complexity of the national market. In the process the power of the local landed interest is inevitably superseded; and these passages, and others like them, testify to the way George Eliot understands that protracted struggle between the landowning interest and the industrial and commercial bourgeoisie to which I referred in the Introductory chapter. These changes provide, moreover, the essential context for understanding the events of the novel. In a famous passage George Eliot writes: 'These social changes in Treby parish are comparatively public matters, and this history is chiefly concerned with the private life of a few men and women; but there is no private life which has not been determined by a wider public life' (*Felix Holt*, ch. 3). This is a very important emphasis, and in one sense the book is written to bear it out, to trace the minute and complex network of this determination. But we are now back to the metaphor of the 'net' and the 'web', and we have seen the radical ambiguity that inheres in that conception of social life.

One aspect of Treby's new participation in the 'wider public life' of the nation is the very fact of a Radical candidate, Harold Transome, fighting an election on national issues. Yet this aspect of the transformation of Treby life is hardly endorsed by George Eliot. It is precisely such a liberal politics, still more a Radical politics, which puts its hope in the machinery of Parliament, against which the book is directed. The novel's title, then—*Felix Holt, the Radical*—is an attempt to effect a redefinition of Radicalism. Felix himself says that he is ' "A Radical,—yes; but I want to go to some roots a good deal lower down than the franchise" ' (*Felix Holt*, ch. 27). To remain obsessed with such questions as the franchise is to be blind to the real determining processes of social change which work through both the transformations in Treby that the novel describes and through the incalculably diffusive action of one person upon another.

If George Eliot's endorsement of the bourgeois transformation of society is seriously qualified, it nevertheless remains the case that the novel amounts to a fundamental rejection of the 'landed interest'. Not only are aristocratic culture and value represented in overwhelmingly hostile ways, but one of the central currents of the book, Esther Lyon's gradual 'conversion' to a sense of higher things, is precisely based upon a rejection of the sterile gentility of Transome Court. It is not in terms of rank and its attractions that the inadequacies of bourgeois political culture are measured; rather they are measured by the novelist's presumed greater knowledge of the real determining springs of social transformation.

The final attitude of the novel to the bourgeois transformation of English society is thus a complex one. In its broad outlines it remains endorsed, though qualified by a nostalgia whose roots are both personal and ideological. Faced with the carrying-forward of that transformation in the 1860s, however, the novel is deeply hostile to the contemporary liberal understanding which seems mistakenly devoted to the arena of public, political life as the means of real social improvement. The conclusion of the novel suggests, with its rather heavy-handed irony, how little real improvement has accompanied material prosperity:

> As to all that wide parish of Treby Magna, it had since prospered as the rest of England has prospered. Doubtless there is more enlightenment now. Whether the farmers are all public-spirited, the shopkeepers nobly independent, the Sproxton men entirely sober and judicious, and the publicans all fit, like Gaius, to be the friends of an apostle—these things I have not heard, not having correspondence in those parts. Whether any presumption may be drawn from the fact that North Loamshire does not yet return a Radical candidate, I leave to the all-wise—I mean the newspapers. (*Felix Holt*, 'Epilogue')

Treby life, in short, has remained little changed in its essentials, though 'doubtless there is more enlightenment now'. George Eliot's problem, as we have seen, is that the inhabitants of Treby scarcely recognise the bearers of enlightenment even when they live there; and she has still more difficulty in imagining ways in which men like Felix and Rufus Lyon can bring their enlightenment profitably to bear upon society at large.

Felix Holt is George Eliot's most insistently anti-political novel. It has been suggested that the characterisation of Will Ladislaw in *Middlemarch* is in part an attempt to envisage a positive version of a political figure to test the limits of this anti-political stance.[6] But in more general terms *Middlemarch* carries forward the logic of both *Romola* and *Felix Holt*, in pitting a degraded social life against individuals of higher and more enlightened capacities; the defeat of both Dorothea and Lydgate suggest the real obstacles that lie in the way of the progress of improvement. *Daniel Deronda* takes this logic still further; in the last novel of her career, George Eliot reasserts the necessity of political commitment, but can find no

79

appropriate channel for it in English life. The England of this novel is one of mannered and cultivated sterility which can find no outlet for the hero's aspirations, which are instead directed to Zionism and a flight from England. It is perhaps the final consequence of the crisis in liberal thought with which we began this chapter; for it points to the ultimately crippling split between the personal and the popular which marks George Eliot's re-ordered aesthetic priorities of the 1860s.

4

Middlemarch: 'Ideally Illuminated Space'

The novel that followed *Felix Holt*, *Middlemarch*, remains in many respects the most ambitious of George Eliot's books. It is ambitious not only in its scope, for it is no less than an attempt at a total representation of a provincial town, but also in its intellectual range. *Middlemarch* is the novel in which George Eliot makes the greatest effort to bring the multifarious narratives and observations which might constitute a 'total representation' into meaningful coherence and order. The book is a massive effort of understanding and of the will to knowledge; it also bears continuous witness to the pains of that effort. This chapter is devoted to some of the implications of George Eliot's attempt to comprehend and make sense of English society at an exemplary moment of transition.

The scope of the novel is, in part, simply a result of the range and diversity of the narratives and characterisations which it weaves together. The book is enormously complex; George Eliot makes great efforts, just at the level of plot, to connect one story with another. This complexity is also, of course, significant; it signifies the mutual dependence of one person on another in society, a point made overtly in the novel:

> But any one watching keenly the stealthy convergence of human lots, sees a slow preparation of effects from one life to another, which tells like a calculated irony on the indifference or the frozen stare with which we look at our unintroduced neighbour. Destiny stands by sarcastic with our *dramatis personae* folded in her hand. (ch. 11)

This can usefully be read as much as a comment on the procedures of the novel itself as a comment on the ironies of destiny. One of the main strategies of the book will be to expose the 'stealthy convergence of human lots'; this is as much a social as a moral interdependence. The massive complexity of the book, its attempt to trace the 'slow preparation of effects' in minute and meticulous detail, makes up a substantial part of what George Eliot means by 'society'.

For all the power of the individual characterisations, then, the object of George Eliot's attention, in *Middlemarch* perhaps more than any of her novels, is a collectivity: English society at a particular and striking moment in its history. In fact it is the same moment of history—the Reform crisis of 1830–32—that provides the setting for *Felix Holt*, and as in the earlier novel there is the same effort to understand the whole movement of a society. The passage I have just quoted continues thus:

> Old provincial society had its share of this subtle movement: had not only its striking downfalls, its brilliant young professional dandies who ended by living up an entry with a drab and six children for their establishment, but also those less marked vicissitudes which are constantly shifting the boundaries of social

intercourse, and begetting new consciousness of inter-dependence. Some slipped a little downward, some got higher footing: people denied aspirates, gained wealth, and fastidious gentlemen stood for boroughs; some were caught in political currents; some in ecclesiastical, and perhpas found themselves surprisingly grouped in consequence; while a few personages or families that stood with rock firmness amid all this fluctuation, were slowly presenting new aspects in spite of solidity, and altering with the double change of self and beholder. Municipal town and rural parish gradually made fresh threads of connection—gradually, as the old stocking gave way to the savings-bank, and the worship of the solar guinea became extinct, while squires and baronets, and even lords who had once lived blamelessly afar from the civic mind, gathered the faultiness of closer acquaintanceship. Settlers, too, came from distant counties, some with an alarming novelty of skill, others with an offensive advantage of cunning. In fact, much the same sort of movement and mixture went on in old England as we find in older Herodotus . . . (ch. 11)

A novel which attempts to bear out this passage, as *Middlemarch* does, will indeed be an extraordinary effort of careful and painstaking construction. But the passage, with its characteristic ironic stress on the less dignified minutiae of life along with the larger movements, is also suggestive of other elements of George Eliot's realism—her confidence in her ability to trace the significance of even the smallest detail, like the attempt to 'deny aspirates'. Even such details as these are symptomatic; they can be placed, accounted for, understood as part of the wider movement of a society at large.

Middlemarch represents, in fact, the most comprehensive development of that aspect of George Eliot's artistic project which is committed to the tracing of cause and effect, because this gives the most solid foothold in the world of the actual. In this the novel stands in strong continuity with all of her work from *Scenes of Clerical Life* onwards, though we have seen that the assessment of ordinary English life changes considerably in the course of her career. *Middlemarch* equally gives powerful expression to another aspect of what I earlier discussed under the heading of the 'extension of our sympathies', for it is in this novel that the most convincing claim is made for the grand aesthetic categories, such as tragedy, to be applied to the ordinary and the everyday. This indeed provokes some of George Eliot's finest writing, as in the following celebrated passage when Dorothea is found weeping on her wedding-trip to Rome:

> Nor can I suppose that when Mrs Casaubon is discovered in a fit of weeping six weeks after her wedding, the situation will be regarded as tragic. Some discouragement, some faintness of heart at the new real future which replaces the imaginary, is not unusual, and we do not expect people to be deeply moved by what is not unusual. That element of tragedy which lies in the very fact of frequency, has not yet wrought itself into the coarse emotion of mankind; and perhaps our frames could hardly bear much of it. If we had a keen vision and feeling of all ordinary human life, it would be like hearing the grass grow and the squirrel's heart beat, and we should die of that roar which lies on the other side of silence. As it is, the quickest of us walk about well wadded with stupidity. (ch. 20)

The claim to tragedy here is powerful, justified by the context and poignantly asserted. It adds a whole new dimension to the extension of sympathy, for that aesthetic, in its first enunciation, seemed almost comfortable; here, feeling joined with insight become both morally essential and potentially overwhelming. It is a powerful and important moment in the novel.

In the face of writing such as this is seems churlish to insist that some of the currents in the novel run counter to this eloquent claim for the inherent dignity of the ordinary. That wise voice that we hear speaking so forcefully about Dorothea's tragedy is heard again on the subject of Mr

Casaubon; but here the claim to tragedy is somewhat more ambivalent:

> To a mind largely instructed in the human destiny hardly anything could be more interesting than the inward conflict implied in [Mr Casaubon's] formal measured address, delivered with the usual sing-song and motion of the head. Nay, are there many situations more sublimely tragic than the struggle of the soul with the demand to renounce a work which has been all the significance of its life—a significance which is to vanish as the waters which come and go where no man has need of them? But there was nothing to strike others as sublime about Mr Casaubon, and Lydgate, who had some contempt at hand for futile scholarship, felt a little amusement mingling with his pity. He was at present too ill acquainted with disaster to enter into the pathos of a lot where everything is below the level of tragedy except the passionate egoism of the sufferer. (ch. 42)

In discussing *The Mill on the Floss* we noticed an ambivalence about whether the novel was to be understood as a tragedy or a tragi-comedy. A similar ambivalence is indicated in this passage. The 'mind largely instructed in the human destiny' can certainly recognise tragedy in Mr Casaubon's situation, despite his pomposity and absurdity. At the end of the passage, however, we are told that 'everything is below the level of tragedy except the passionate egoism of the sufferer; and this is an equally authoritative judgement, it is not only Lydgate's. The doctor's own attitude does exactly catch the ambivalence, however. The amusement that mingles with his pity—one of the fit emotions for tragedy since Aristotle—is just what prevents him from perceiving Casaubon as tragic; it is matched by the ironic distance which persistently separates the narrator from the characters during the novel.

There are, of course, many other useful comparisons to be made with the earlier novels. One that is especially illuminating is the way that the representation of the provincial middle class has been transformed since *Adam Bede* and *The Mill on the Floss*. Earlier, I argued that in *Adam Bede* George Eliot represented that part of the provincial middle class typified by Adam himself and the Poysers in such a way as to demonstrate her confidence for the future in their working-day habits and values. In *The Mill on the Floss*, by contrast, despite some countervailing efforts, the habits and values of the Dodsons and Tullivers seemed constricting, ossified and sterile. In *Middlemarch*, this split reappears within the novel itself. It is the Garths, most especially Caleb Garth, who continue the tradition of Adam Bede; it is the Featherstones and their various connections who represent the most sharply hostile version of the acquisitive yeoman-farmer. The split between these two aspects of the provincial middle class indicates most sharply George Eliot's difficulty in retaining a confident appraisal of middle-class values rooted in the realities of their work and economic position.

It is not hard to see that the Garths represent a strongly positive version of certain middle-class values: self-respect, hard work, thrift, modest worldly success. The continuity with Adam Bede is clear: ' "I think any hardship is better than pretending to do what one is paid for, and never really doing it" ' (ch. 14), Mary Garth remarks, and the comment exactly catches that belief in doing a job well to which George Eliot is so committed. Caleb Garth's notion of 'business' equally encapsulates this ethic; business for him means having a love and pride in your work whatever that work is. This indeed is his practical religion, in a way reminiscent of Adam Bede: 'it would be difficult to convey to those who never heard him utter the word "business", the peculiar tone of fervid veneration, of religious regard, in which he wrapped it, as a consecrated symbol is wrapped in its gold-fringed linen' (ch. 24). Yet the condition of his maintaining his dignity is that his notion of 'business' should exclude the actual earning of money, which is a secondary and rather sordid accident of his work. His rejection of Bulstrode's employment when he learns the tainted source of the banker's wealth demonstrates what the separation of 'business' from 'money' means: the cost of Caleb Garth's retaining George Eliot's whole-hearted respect is that she should be able to distinguish the material transformation of the world for the better which he accomplishes, from the economic relations which in fact make such a labour possible. (George Eliot tries to make this a distinction between honest and ill-gotten wealth. This is why Bulstrode has a past, as a pawnbroker and receiver, that comes out of the exciting low-life novels which George Eliot despised. The formal break from the sober realism which elsewhere dominates the text indicates her difficulty in maintaining a distinction which cannot be maintained in the realities of market relations.)

By contrast with the Garths, the Featherstones and the Waules represent an extemely hostile version of those qualities which are treated rather more ambivalently in the Dodsons of *The Mill on the Floss*. Their obsession with money matters, their peasant selfishness and suspicion, contrast markedly with the principled practicality of the Garths. Indeed, one of the most striking and worked for moments in the novel is when Mary Garth rejects old Peter Featherstone's attempt to involve her in altering his will on his death-bed; Book Three, 'Waiting for Death', culminates with the impressive, even melodramatic moral tableau of Peter 'dead, with his right hand clasping the keys, and his left hand lying on the heap of notes and gold' (ch. 33). The scene asks to be read as testimony of the ultimate impotence of cash over those who have a higher standard within.

Thus the split between the Garths and the Featherstones represents a split between different aspects of provincial middle-class values held triumphantly together in the representation of the Bedes and the Poysers; and it is a split which is caused by the inability or unwillingness on George

Eliot's part to recognise the economic basis of the labour of men like Caleb Garth—necessarily mediated through money. In fact the attitude to money, which plays so important a part in the novel, is itself a complex one. There is no doubt that George Eliot remains deeply committed to the thrifty, hard-working and self-helping values of people like the Garths; her commitment is equally evident in her criticism of the Vincy's extravagant housekeeping or, more importantly, in her criticism of Lydgate. One of his 'spots of commonness', which prevent him from fulfilling his high ambitions as a doctor, is his aristocratic disdain for thrift in the common objects of life (the meaning of the word 'common' shifts widely and symptomatically in the course of George Eliot's career.[1] It is itself, of course, a word heavily loaded with class connotations). There are innumerable similar indications of George Eliot's commitment to thrift. Yet Featherstone's obsession with money as an expression of his power and egoism is, obviously enough, thoroughly disgusting, and we are equally to admire Will's proud rejection of Bulstrode's cash and Caleb Garth's rejection of Bulstrode as an employer. One of the things which the novel is to teach us (as Dorothea, indeed, promises to learn when she finally commits herself to Will) is 'what everything costs'. A fit estimate of the importance of cash is an important social and moral indicator throughout the book.

So the pictures of the provincial middle class in *Middlemarch* are marked by a series of splits which testify to the intractability of market and financial relations to favourable representation. In the Garths we can perhaps see George Eliot making amends to English provincial life after its almost exclusively hostile representation in *Felix Holt*. Yet they remain an exception in *Middlemarch*, which substantially continues the overwhelming sense of ignorance, stupidity and triviality which its predecessor suggested were the main characteristics of provincial life. *Middlemarch* is precisely addressed to the possibilities of 'enlightenment' and real progress (based on scientific knowledge) in a world substantially hostile to them. It is impossible to read the novel at all sympathetically without being infuriated at the ignorant and prejudiced resistance to Lydgate, the offensive and narrow-minded estimations of Dorothea, and the bigoted assessments of Will Ladislaw. All these characters are engaged in one aspect or another of the project of enlightenment. Dorothea's religious energy is devoted to '"widening the skirts of light and making the struggle with darkness narrower"' (ch. 39). Will, engaged on political reform which a later and wiser generation will judge less enthusiastically, is nevertheless satisfied that he is working 'no meaner engine than knowledge' (ch. 51). Lydgate's whole position as the failed hero of the novel is based on his commitment to science and his unique position as a doctor in putting science to practical, ameliorative effect. Yet Lydgate's defeat, and Dorothea's partial defeat and her flight from Middlemarch with Will, testify to the finally victorious power of ignorance and small-mindedness.

If there is no point in underlining George Eliot's endorsement of Lydgate's high ideals, it is well worth emphasising her endorsement of Dorothea's idealism. For there has been a persistent strain of criticism, starting perhaps with Mrs Cadwallader, which has sought to belittle and denigrate Dorothea's dissatisfaction with things as they are—and her search for something better—in the name of varying kinds of accommodation to the actual. One line of criticism, most trenchantly expressed by Leavis, recognises that George Eliot does endorse Dorothea's idealism but finds this an embarrassing flaw in the novel. Another line tries to elevate the short-term ironies against Dorothea in the early part of the novel into a considered judgement and 'placing' of the character.[2] Both are strategies aimed at deadening the radical impact of a heroine who is uncompromising in her rejection of the gratifications of wealth and genteel femininity—a rejection that fits uncomfortably with a 'maturity' that such critics are keen to promote. In the following chapter we shall examine more closely the constrictions of genteel femininity, especially in relation to *Daniel Deronda*. Here, we can observe that while it might be the case that the character is idealised (in the sense outlined in the previous chapter, in that it is difficult to account for her nobility in concrete social and historical terms), it nevertheless remains the case that her idealism is endorsed, even celebrated. Despite her inability to see that Casaubon is a soulless pedant or that some of her 'notions' are naive, Dorothea remains a character who embodies the hopes for humanity's future.

This, then, is the ultimate context of her partial defeat. You can best get a sense of George Eliot's determination to see at least some beneficial value from a life like Dorothea's by looking again at the two final paragraphs of the Epilogue. One of the stiking aspects of *Middlemarch* is its capacity to dramatise the 'imperfect social state' which is the immediate cause of Dorothea's defeat; the novel might be said to be dominated by fear and frustration at the power of ignorance and triviality. Lydgate's disgust that ' "it seems as if the paltry fellows were always to turn the scale" ', for all its arrogance of expression, nevertheless remains the central anxiety of the book.

For we need to take very seriously that sentence in the novel's 'Prelude' which speaks of the absence of a 'coherent social faith and order' as an explanation of why people like Dorothea could not—here, now, in the nineteenth century— live a heroic life like the life of St Theresa. Her history, and indeed Lydgate's, is to be explained by the fact that Middlemarch (or more generally, English society in the earlier nineteenth century) lacks a coherent social faith and order that could translate her noble aspirations into noble deeds. A passage later in the novel, which again refers to St

Theresa, indicates what this absence implies for Dorothea:

> She did not want to deck herself with knowledge—to wear it loose from the nerves and blood that fed her action; and if she had written a book she must have done it as St Theresa did, under the command of an authority that constrained her conscience. But something she yearned for by which her life might be filled with action at once rational and ardent; and since the time was gone by for guiding visions and spiritual directors, since prayer heightened yearning but not instruction, what lamp was there but knowledge? Surely learned men kept the only oil; and who more learned than Mr Casaubon? (ch. 10)

The only irony here is directed at the last sentence. A coherent social faith is one that would enable the transition from the personal to the general good for which Dorothea yearns; it would provide a knowledge that would integrate all her faculties, emotional as well as intellectual, and ensure a further integration of her whole personality in the onward life of society. The implicit model of such a faith is Catholicism in the Middle Ages—only implicit here but made explicit throughout Comte's writings of whose conclusions this passage is an eloquent summation. For this passage is addressed to what George Eliot, after Comte, sees as the central dilemma of the nineteenth century (and as far as the analysis is true at all, it equally applies to the twentieth century): How are we to find a knowledge which can replace religion as a coherent and integrative social faith? For in the absence of such a knowledge, individuals, and with them society, are condemned to a sense of frustration and isolation.

However powerful this implied ideal of knowledge, you might not find it altogether attractive: knowledge is conceived here as a commanding authority rather than an enabling or liberating capacity. Yet it is certainly one ideal of knowledge to which the book aspires, and it is the scientific knowledge that Lydgate is extending which might substitute for the 'knowledge' of religion. His failure points to that other great deficiency in Middlemarch, which accompanies the absence of a coherent social faith: the absence of a coherent social order. This indeed is the misfortune of this society. The relations that subsist between people are not of that permanancy which would be guaranteed by a social order—the people who might provide authority are almost as ignorant and misguided as the rest. Brooke, Chettam, the various priests in the novel, Bulstrode (bankers were to play a leading role in Comte's positivist Utopia) all fail, for one reason or another, to provide the leadership that might bind society together. While this is an analysis of society which recognises the inadequacy of liberal social ideals, according to which enlightened self-interest provides sufficient social binding, in its nostalgia for order and authority we can recognise a powerful element of conservatism.

So *Middlemarch* carries forward many elements of George Eliot's earlier novels; indeed, it gives the most powerful and eloquent expression to that element of her aesthetic which asserts the intrinsic dignity of the everyday and the ordinary. Yet the novel combines this assertion, in a way which potentially runs counter to it, with a predominantly hostile assessment of English provincial life, despite the novelist's commitment to a middle-class ethic of thrift and work which is one of the central strands of that life. Above all, the novel is pessimistic about the possibilities for enlightenment, carried forward and enlarged by all the central, positive characters of the book. So we are left with what superficially appears a paradox. The novel which is most confident about its own capacity to bring the enormously complex representation of provincial society into coherence and order is also the most pessimistic about the coherence and order of that society itself.

II

This paradox is worth pursuing. Let us start with a comment from Sidney Colvin, who reviewed the book sympathetically shortly after its appearance in 1873. He wrote of George Eliot:

> the general definition of her work, I should say, is precisely this—that among writers of the imagination, she has taken the lead in expressing and discussing the lives and ways of common folks . . . in terms of scientific thought and the positive synthesis.. . . Thus there is the most pointed contrast between the matter of these English tales and the manner of their telling. The matter is antiquated in our recollections, the manner seems to anticipate the future of our thoughts.[3]

This description is substantially correct. As we saw earlier with *Romola* (though it is true of all the novels) *Middlemarch* emerges from the gap in knowledge between its characters and its narrator. As Colvin suggests, this is partly just a matter of historical distance: people in 1830 were simply incapable of knowing the things that people knew in 1870. But more importantly, people from the earlier period could not conceive of the *kind* of knowledge ('the positive synthesis') which was later to become available. So it is not just a matter of the accumulation of knowledge, for science (including, of course, the science of society) does not progress simply by finding out more and more. It is rather that the science of the later nineteenth century is capable of understanding and explaining the people of an earlier period. The knowledge of now can place, identify and see round the knowledge of then. It can explain both what people believed they knew and what they didn't know; both their knowledge and their ignorance.

Fortunately, George Eliot gives us an excellent account of how she conceives the scientific imagination—the basis of reliable knowledge—in her account of Lydgate's method of research:

> Many men have been praised as vividly imaginative on the strength of their profuseness in indifferent drawing or cheap narration . . . . But these kinds of inspiration Lydgate regarded as rather vulgar and vinous compared with the imagination that reveals subtle actions inaccessible by any sort of lens, but tracked in that outer darkness through long pathways of necessary sequence by the inward light which is the last refinement of Energy, capable of bathing even the ethereal atoms in its ideally illuminated space. (ch. 16)

This is not just an account of the scientific imagination; it effectively describes the kind of knowledge to which the novel itself aspires.[4] *Middlemarch* the novel is produced by bringing light to bear upon Middlemarch the town; the novel resembles the 'ideally illuminated space' in which Lydgate gains access to his biological truth. The power of thought, of ideal conceptions, is necessary for an understanding of the real: the various narratives and characterisations which make up Middlemarch the town do not speak their own meaning but need to be organised, dwelt upon or generalised from, for their significance to be made apparent.

The high proportion of commentary to story in the novel is thus a function of this effort to locate and understand English provincial life and the movement of its history. I use 'story' here to mean more than just the sequence of events in the novel; it denotes the sum of the characters and events as they are supposed to have occurred in the novel's time and place. To know about these as readers we have to be told: there is no story without a story-teller, no narrative without narration. Narration, of course, is not confined to commentary; its presence can be traced in a variety of features of the text: its pace of telling, the extent to which the reader is given access to the full facts of character or event, significant comparisons or juxtapositions, the ironic distance from or empathetic solidarity with what the characters say or do. *Middlemarch* is marked by its high proportion of commentary, which we can define as those sections of the text which stand outside its story and whose authoritative status we do not question—I have quoted several examples already in this chapter. But the novel is also marked by the complexity with which it interweaves commentary and story. Story in my definition includes what the characters say and think; and it is always important to disentangle what is the character's speech and what the narrator's. Many passages of the novel are marked by a complex irony which often works against the characters but which can modulate into agreement or solidarity; such passages require a reading continually alert to the level of authority which any sentence or phrase enjoys.

Let us take the following passage, predominantly of commentary, as an example; it occurs at an early stage of Rosamond's flirtation with Lydgate, when she has already begun to indulge in daydreams about a marriage 'establishment':

> But Rosamond was not one of those helpless girls who betray themselves unawares, and whose behaviour is awkwardly driven by their impulses, instead of being steered by wary grace and propriety. Do you imagine that her rapid forecast and rumination concerning house-furniture and society were ever discernible in her conversation, even with her mamma? On the contrary, she would have expressed the prettiest surprise and disapprobation if she had heard that another young lady had been detected in that immodest prematureness—indeed, would probably have disbelieved in its possibility. For Rosamond never showed any unbecoming knowledge, and was always that combination of correct sentiments, music, dancing, drawing, elegant note-writing, private album for extracted verse, and perfect blond loveliness, which made the irresistible woman for the doomed man of that date. Think no unfair evil of her, pray:

she had no wicked plots, nothing sordid or mercenary; in fact, she never thought of money except as something necessary which other people would always provide. She was not in the habit of devising falsehoods, and if her statements were no direct clue to fact, why, they were not intended in that light—they were among her elegant accomplishments, intended to please. Nature had inspired many arts in finishing Mrs Lemon's favourite pupil, who by general consent (Fred's excepted) was a rare compound of beauty, cleverness, and amiability. (ch. 27)

This is a passage of commentary that carries within it many of the judgements and vocabulary of the story; they are held in an ironic suspension which enables the reader to 'place' them. Thus, in the third sentence, Rosamond's hypothetical surprise and disapprobation could only be 'pretty' to those who believe that girls should be modest and innocently uncalculating; her sentiments are indeed 'correct', but only because the society 'of that date' deemed them to be so: the narrator and thus the reader can see the inadequacy of that correctness. Rosamond's 'perfect blond loveliness', or later, her being a 'rare compound of beauty, cleverness and amiability', are the judgements of the normative voice of Middlemarch (its 'general consent'); the irony that plays about such phrases testifies to the narrator's ability to judge more adequately not only Rosamond's merits but more generally on what constitutes a noble ideal of womanhood.

Implicit within this passage, then, is a feature which is characteristic of the novel as a whole: that there are different levels of understanding and vocabulary, and that the highest level is that of the narrator. It is useful to describe the conjunction of 'understanding and vocabulary' as 'discourse', a term with at least two advantages. First, it suggests the inextricability of understanding from the vocabulary in which it is expressed: all languages, from natural ones like English or Italian to the highly specialised jargons of science, the tabloid press or CB radio, cut up the world in particular ways and thus shape their users' understandings. Secondly, since discourse is necessarily shared between people, to use the term suggests its social or interpersonal character: discourse is not originated by an individual but is the characteristic language of a group or class. *Middlemarch*, therefore, is made up of a hierarchy of discourses, with the discourse of the narrator at the top of the pile.[5]

A discursive hierarchy is not just a feature of *Middlemarch*: it is the defining feature of the realist text. Such a text is marked by the desire to place or define the discourses of those who inhabit the story, by means of the superior discourses of the story-teller, which in so far as it *can* place or define other discourses, remains itself unplaced or undefined. It is the last characteristic which defines such a text as realist: the discourse of the narrator refuses to recognise itself as discourse and therefore claims that it speaks the truth unproblematically, claiming the capacity to define the real. Moreover, *Middlemarch* does not only do this inadvertently, as innumerable other realist texts do. As we have seen, it does so explicitly and insistently, for George Eliot is emphatic on the inadequacies of most of the discourse of her story. *Middlemarch*, in fact, is not only a discursive hierarchy by virtue of its construction; it insists upon the necessity of maintaining a discursive hierarchy in life.

Let us take as an example the scene at Mrs Dollop's public house, in Book Seven, when gossip about the death of Raffles is beginning to circulate to the detriment of Bulstrode and Lydgate:

> But this vague conviction of indeterminable guilt, which was enough to keep up much head-shaking and biting innuendo even among substantial professional seniors, had for the general mind all the superior power of mystery over fact. Everybody liked better to conjecture how the thing was, than simply to know it; for conjecture soon became more confident than knowledge, and had a more liberal allowance for the incompatible. Even the

97

more definite scandal concerning Bulstrode's earlier life was, for some minds, melted into the mass of mystery, as so much lively metal to be poured out in dialogue, and to take such fantastic shapes as heaven pleased.

This was the tone of thought chiefly sanctioned by Mrs Dollop, the spirited landlady of the Tankard in Slaughter Lane, who had often to resist the shallow pragmatism of customers disposed to think that their reports from the outer world were of equal force with what had 'come up' in her mind. How it had been brought to her she didn't know, but it was there before her as if it had been scored with the chalk on the chimney-board—'as Bulstode should say, his inside was *that black* as if the hairs of his head knowed the thoughts of his heart, he'd tear 'em up by the roots'.

'That's odd,' said Mr Limp, a meditative shoemaker, with weak eyes and a piping voice. 'Why, I read in the *Trumpet* that was what the Duke of Wellington said when he turned his coat and went over to the Romans.'

'Very like,' said Mrs Dollop. 'If one raskill said it, it's more reason why another should. But hypo*crite* as he's been, and holding things with that high hand, as there was no parson i' the country good enough for him, he was forced to take Old Harry into his counsel, and Old Harry's been too many for him.'

'Ay, ay, he's a 'complice you can't send out o' the country,' said Mr. Crabbe the glazier, who gathered much news and groped among it dimly. 'But by what I can make out, there's them says Bulstrode was for running away, for fear o' being found out, before now.' (ch. 71)

A passage such as this demonstrates the characteristics of a discursive hierarchy especially clearly. The words within the quotation marks can be seen to be discourse, placeable and easily accounted for, by their 'deviant' grammatical features. We do not read such speeches for their truth, but for what they tell us about the 'general mind'. Because of this, because we do not 'see through' this language to a reality that it denotes, the speech of these characters is opaque, and their language is to be relished by the reader as examples of the kind of thing such people say. Their opacity is indicated not only by the lightly suggested dialect, but also by such details as the italicising of the last half of the word hypocrite when Mrs Dollop uses it, which draws attention to the way she speaks and not what she says. By contrast, the framing discourse of the narrator is transparent, for it can speak the truth of the characters' discourse; it has the concepts and vocabulary to explain and account for the 'deviant' discourse of the 'general mind'.

A discursive hierarchy is just as much a feature of *Adam Bede* as it is of *Middlemarch*, of course; Mrs Poyser's speech, which is pithy, forceful and witty, is as much to be relished as speech as Mrs Dollop's, though the relish is of a less contemptuous kind. Mrs Poyser's speech can equally be accounted for: we are to accept Mr Irwine's explanation of it as the kind of wit which originates proverbs. The hostility to Mrs Dollop's speech indicates, evidently, the distance which George Eliot has travelled from her earlier happy solidarity with many aspects of common and ordinary life. Even without this overt hostility, however, the novel would still be made up of different discourses, each with different capacities for articulating the truth, and thus each more or less opaque in the way that I have described. However, this is not just an abstract question of different ways of gaining access to the truth; these different discourses are also different class dialects. So what is at stake here is an implicit assertion of the superiority of one class dialect over another.

I suggested earlier that the high proportion of commentary in *Middlemarch* is a function of the effort to locate and understand English provincial life and the movement of a society. We can now begin to see what the implications of such an effort are, and they are perhaps not all attractive ones. If we ask how we are to understand the 'general mind' of Middlemarch, the scene at Mrs Dollop's in part affords the answer: the general mind is characterised by its failure to be scientific: 'Everybody liked better to conjecture how the thing was, than simply to know it.' The general mind is simply incapable of sustaining the sequence of inferences that Lydgate can manage; it is anyway insufficiently impressed by the intractability of facts. The conclusion to be drawn from this, indeed, is precisely not that more general enlightenment can be produced by careful education or explanation, for that too has its pitfalls. George Eliot writes: 'But let the wise be warned against too great readiness at explanation: it multiplies the sources of mistake, lengthening the sum for reckoners sure to go wrong' (ch. 45). The only guarantee for the proper operation of knowledge as a social power is when it can be enforced; it is an aspect of the incoherent social faith and order of Middlemarch that there is no conceivable agency for its enforcement.

George Eliot takes one feature of the realist text, then—the fact that it is built on a discursive hierarchy—and inflects it in a particularly authoritarian direction. Of course, there are elements in the novel which work in the opposite direction. Not all the characters' language provokes the kind of contemptuous humour provided by Mrs Dollop and her customers. Quite apart from the language of Dorothea and Will—which anyway is sufficiently similar to the narrator's own language for it to have the status of truth—one could point to the pleasure provided by Mr Borthrop Trumbull. There is a real affectionate delight and capacity for fun evinced in the display of his magnificent amplifications. More seriously, there is the fine moment in Chapter 56, when the rustics of Frick chase off the railway surveyors, and then refuse to be cajoled by Caleb Garth; Timothy Cooper has an unanswerable rejoinder to Garth's oratory when he says that '"An' so it'll be wi' the railroads. They'll on'y leave the poor man further behind".' This provokes the following:

Caleb was in a difficulty known to any person attempting in dark times and unassisted by miracle to reason with rustics who are in possession of an undeniable truth which they know through a hard process of feeling, and can let it fall like a giant's club on your neatly-carved argument for a social benefit which they do *not* feel. (ch. 56)

This moment is so powerful because Caleb's difficulty in explanation is not caused by an unwillingness to multiply the causes of mistake (which would take us back to the authoritarian problem of man-management) but because he encounters a power of articulate experience which resists assimilation and explanation by his own or the narrator's discourse. Yet this remains a *moment* in the novel; it marks a limit to the confident subordination of other discourses rather than demonstrating a consistent practice of over-turning the authority of the narrator's discourse. By and large, that authority remains unchallenged because to challenge it would overturn the whole novel – or indeed, any realist novel.

Middlemarch, it thus appears, demonstrates a will to knowledge which has some unattractive features. We need to be clear what the presence of commentary—the most overt feature of the discursive hierarchy that makes up the novel— implies. It does not imply that what I have called the story is primary and that the commentary is secondary, though unfortunately the very word 'commentary' tends to suggest this. A number of related nineteenth-and twentieth-century critical positions have sought to elevate story over commentary, by insisting that novels should 'show' rather than 'tell'; or that you should 'trust the tale and not the teller'. Such positions imply both that representations speak their own meaning and that we can deduce their significance unproblematically. In fact, as I have suggested, it is the very instability of meanings carried by representations that continually enforces the necessity for commentary; George Eliot's fullness of comment implies not only an anxiety to enforce appropriate interpretation but equally a readiness to make the grounds of her judgement explicit. Related contemporary versions of such positions have reacted entirely against realism. They tend to play off the realist novel against modernist texts which subvert the very possibility of representation, thus condemning realist novels for a kind of naivety. The argument runs like this: in refusing to recognise that no discourse can be privileged since all discourses are equally socially produced and equally flawed as knowledge, the realist novel is naive in assuming the privileged adequacy of the dominant discourse.[6] The difficulty with this latter position is that it is ultimately cripplingly sceptical. If all discourse is equal and equally inadequate, then we can abandon the effort to understand and explain society; and in doing so we relinquish all hope of purposeful intervention in society. What the fullness of commentary in *Middlemarch* finally testifies to, is George Eliot's refusal to abandon the effort of understanding; and in doing so she keeps open, however slightly, and with whatever qualifications and confusions, the possibility of purposeful intervention in the world she inhabits.

So, in pursuing the implications of the discursive hierarchy, most overt in *Middlemarch*, we have finally to confront a dilemma. On the one hand is George Eliot's wholly admirable desire to understand the past of the society she lives in, to find the right terms to explain it, and to locate the strands of continuity from the past to the present which can be built upon for the future. Yet a condition of this effort of understanding seems to be a distance from, even at times a contempt for, the forms of understanding and the language of ordinary people. In trying to come to terms with the weight and complexity of *Middlemarch*, you need to decide which way you jump when confronted by this dilemma—towards a language of understanding, involving perhaps alienation, or towards the reassurance and solidarity of ordinary language, entailing perhaps confusion about the world you live in and thus impotence to act upon it. Dorothea's sense of alienation, when she realises Casaubon's inadequacy as a source of real knowledge or enlightenment, can be seen as a projection of someone living this dilemma in its full intensity: 'All existence seemed to beat with a lower pulse than her own, and her religious faith was a solitary cry, the struggle out of a nightmare in which every object was writhing and shrinking away from her' (ch. 28).

III

So far in this chapter we have principally been concerned with the relationship between the novel and the world it seeks to represent: English provincial society around 1830, which, through various metonymic devices, appears as the 'story' in *Middlemarch*. Making due allowances for these devices, which means making due allowance for the fact that the 'story' is fiction, we can nevertheless describe the relationship between novel and world as 'referential'. The novel refers to, is in many ways 'about', a world which is independent of the novel; in talking of any novel's 'realism' we are asserting something about its referential function. However, novels—and indeed all language—have two other dominant functions. In so far as writing is produced by an author, with whatever displacements, it works expressively. In so far as it is directed towards a reader it works rhetorically. The famous and commonsensical question which can be asked about all utterances—who is saying what to whom?—is thus a question about the expressive, referential and rhetorical functions in turn. However, we need to go on at once from this simple description of linguistic functions to notice that they do not simply coexist, but are all in a state of tension. In particular, the rhetorical function of language can bracket or undermine its referential function.

It is certainly the case with George Eliot's writing that its set towards the world is subordinate to its set towards the reader. The very notion of the 'extension of sympathy', as we saw in Chapter 2, puts the highest value on changes to be wrought in the reader's mind and character; it is because of this high responsibility that the novelist must provide 'true' representations of popular life. This general subordination of the referential to the rhetorical, moreover, points to an important feature of George Eliot's conception of knowledge: it should be knowledge for use, and should contribute to the general good and not be abstract or sterile pedantry. Dorothea's assimilation of knowledge, her hope that it might lead to action 'at once rational and ardent' (ch. 10), thus provides the highest possible ideal of what knowledge should be; it can direct and support the good life. George Eliot's novels are all directed to bolstering the reader's capacity to lead the good life.

It is for this reason that the shape of a George Eliot paragraph or chapter is often a rhetorical one, carefully shifting from the particular to the general and back again to find the inclusive generality which will both place the story and enforce the reader's recognition, solidarity or indignation. The end of Chapter 6, which recounts Sir James Chettam's disappointment at learning of Dorothea's engagement to Casaubon, provides an example where the chapter culminates in the generalising and inclusive comment:

> We mortals, men and women, devour many a disappointment between breakfast and dinner-time; keep back the tears and look a little pale about the lips, and in answer to inquiries say, 'Oh, nothing!' Pride helps us; and pride is not a bad thing when it only urges us to hide our own hurts—not to hurt others. (ch. 6)

Whatever we may think of the wisdom of this, its placing in the chapter is what is interesting here. The comment rounds off the chapter with a generality in which the reader is included, reinforced by having Sir James' experience offered as representative of his or her own experience—indeed, as the experience of all humanity. The chapter is shaped, in other words, to culminate in a generality to which the reader's assent is assumed. The representation of Chettam is subordinate to or serves this rhetorical purpose.

This is an especially overt example; even, perhaps, with that sudden introduction of the too generally inclusive 'we mortals', rather a clumsy one. As often, the generality precedes its instances so that they serve as illustrations; or a paragraph will shift from one level to another intricately and persistently:

> Lydgate, certain that his patient wished to be alone, soon left him; and the black figure with hands behind and head bent forward continued to pace the walk where the dark yew-trees gave him a mute companionship in melancholy, and the little shadows of bird or leaf that fleeted across the isles of sunlight, stole along in silence as in the presence of a sorrow. Here was a man who now for the first time found himself looking into the eyes of death—who was passing through one of those rare moments of experience when we feel the truth of a commonplace, which is as different from what we call knowing it, as the vision of waters upon the earth is different from the delirious vision of the water which cannot be had to cool the burning tongue. When the commonplace 'We must all die' transforms itself suddenly into the acute consciousness 'I must die—and soon', then death grapples us, and his fingers are cruel; afterwards, he may come to fold us in his arms as our mother did, and our last moment of dim earthly discerning may be like the first. To Mr Casaubon now, it was as if he suddenly found himself on the dark river-brink and heard the plash of the oncoming oar, not discerning the forms, but expecting the summons. In such an hour the mind does not change its lifelong

bias, but carries it onwards in imagination to the other side of death, gazing backward—perhaps with the divine calm of beneficence, perhaps with the petty anxieties of self-assertion. What was Mr Casaubon's bias his acts will give us a clue to. He held himself to be, with some private scholarly reservations, a believing Christian, as to estimates of the present and hopes of the future. But what we strive to gratify, though we may call it a distant hope, is an immediate desire; the future estate for which men drudge up city alleys exists already in their imagination and love. And Mr Casaubon's immediate desire was not for divine communion and light divested of earthly conditions; his passionate longings, poor man, clung low and mist-like in very shady places. (ch. 42)

The shifts from story to commentary here are especially intricate. The first sentence belongs to the story; its specificity of detail, though it has some atmospheric significance ('as in the presence of sorrow'), is more motivated by the desire to give the effect of reality, guaranteed by the very superfluousness of the detail. The beginning of the second sentence, however, shifts the writing into commentary; the phrase 'here was a man' locates Casaubon as an example, introduced in a specific relationship of place and time to both writer and reader. In fact the exemplary quality of Mr Casaubon's experience is established by the use of such words as 'here', 'those', 'such', and by the use of the definite or indefinite article. (Such words are technically classified as 'deixis', from the Greek for 'pointing'. They locate any utterance in time and place with regard to the subject of the utterance.) The passage switches momentarily back into story with the sentence beginning: 'To Mr Casaubon now . . .', but then back into commentary with the phrase 'in such an hour'. The remainder of the passage switches from one to the other with every sentence, ending with a sentence of story, though the phrase 'poor man' allows the reader to resume the perspective of commentary.

This intricate shifting of narrative levels, however, is of especial interest as an instance of rhetoric. The shift from story to commentary also involves the inclusion of the reader in the 'wise' perspective which can place Mr Casaubon's experience, and see in it both those elements which give it the dignity of powerful human experience, and those which make him exemplary of the 'lifelong bias' of the mind. The use of the personal pronouns 'we', 'our' and 'us' is obviously especially important in reaching out and including the reader in the perspective of the narrator. So the same movement which establishes the type of reference of the passage (Mr Casaubon's typicality), also establishes the reader in a relationship of pitying solidarity with that reference. But it is the second relationship which justifies or gives point to the first—there is no point in writing about Mr Casaubon unless as readers we can be brought into this relationship with his experience, and thus made better prepared to confront our own.

Both these examples have insisted on the solidarity of reader and character on the widest possible basis—on their common mortality. Throughout the novel, however, the reader is invited by the text to take up a variety of different positions; to the extent that we read the novel sympathetically, we are successively situated as dispassionate observers, solitary sufferers, amused and ironic overseers, and any variety and combination of these positions. Such positions in her readers are the ultimate *raison d'etre* of George Eliot's novels; she is finally anxious that her books should reinforce socially and 'humanly' positive attitudes in their readers, and should combat those attitudes which make for unhappiness and anti-social egoism. This ambition subsumes all the ironies and all the sympathy of her writing; it is to this ambition that all her representations are finally subordinate.

5

'A Woman's Life'

I

This final chapter focuses on *Daniel Deronda*. In connection principally with this novel, I discuss a central and important topic, that has so far been postponed from chapter to chapter—the whole question of gender in George Eliot's writing. This is handled in complex and even contradictory ways in the novels, and requires us to extend our notion of 'discursive hierarchy' as I have outlined it. First, however, it would be as well briefly to indicate the place of *Daniel Deronda* in the trajectory of George Eliot's whole career.

Daniel Deronda, George Eliot's last completed novel, at first seems very different from all the novels that precede it. For one thing, it is a novel of contemporary life, set in the 1860s only ten years before its date of composition. All the previous novels, as we have seen, were set in the past. If they posed the question, 'How did we get from there to here?', *Daniel Deronda* takes this question a big step forward to ask, 'Where do we go now?' Secondly, this novel is set much more exclusively than the previous novels in the milieu of the English governing class. In so far as it is concerned with popular life, it is no longer the popular life of England but the popular life of the Jews. Both these important differences mean that there is less of a gap between narrator and characters than in any of the previous novels, with important consequences for the kind of narrative authority the novel enjoys. Finally, and perhaps most surprisingly, the novel seems to endorse politics albeit in a conditional and peculiar way: at the end of the book Daniel Deronda leaves England to begin a work of national regeneration for the Jews. He passes into history, in other words, unlike Felix Holt or Dorothea Brooke whose destinies only run to 'unhistoric acts'.

Yet despite these substantial differences, the novel continues essentially the same logic that had been established in the earlier books. For all that *Daniel Deronda* is set in large part in the world of the English governing class, it remains fundamentally hostile to that class—the book contains the last of George Eliot's portraits of landed society, and it is at once tolerant, good-humoured and damning. Mr Gascoigne, Sir Hugh Mallinger, Mr Bult, all typify in their different ways the comfortable worldliness of high Victorian England, summed up perhaps by Mr Bult, who 'had the general solidity and suffusive pinkness of a healthy Briton on the central table-land of life' (*Daniel Deronda*, ch. 22). All are measured by the musician Klesmer, who speaks of the 'lack of idealism' in English politics, and who is indignant that in England all political questions should be reduced to the commercial one of 'Buy cheap and sell dear'. Still more importantly, the world of these men—self-confident, complacent, successful at managing affairs—this world is finally measured by Daniel Deronda's decision, after he has spent most of the book in search of a vocation, to quit it for the East.

This very decision points to another important continuity from the earlier books. We have seen that a persistent difficulty for George Eliot has been to provide a social or historical setting that could account for the central positive characters in the novels—an idealisation of character that compensated for a diminished confidence in English popular life reaching back at least as early as *The Mill on the Floss*. This difficulty persists with the characterisation of Daniel, though some effort is made to account for the generally sympathetic and slightly melancholic cast of his character by his boyhood shame at his suspected illegitimacy. *Daniel Deronda*, however, finally resolves the split between character and environment, but in a way which points directly away from any prospect of English national regeneration. For both the mystery of Daniel's powerful if indiscriminate capacity for sympathy, and his destiny in furthering human progress, are solved by the discovery of his Jewish ancestry:

> It was as if he had found an added soul in finding his ancestry— his judgement no longer wandering in the mazes of impartial sympathy, but choosing, with that partiality which is man's best strength, the closer fellowship that makes sympathy practical— exchanging that bird's eye reasonableness which soars to avoid preference and loses all sense of quality for the generous reasonableness of drawing shoulder to shoulder with men of like inheritence. (*Daniel Deronda*, ch. 63)

The Jewish race, in other words, can provide a 'coherent social faith and order', and it can provide a context for action 'at once rational and ardent'; it was the absence of these conditions, we recall, that determined Dorothea's failure to become a St Theresa. Daniel's discovery of his Jewishness, in fact, and his decision to quit England, are the final results of that split which had fissured George Eliot's writing: between character and environment, organism and its medium, or between the ideal and the real. This split can only be resolved, it seems, outside the prosperous but sterile milieu of mid-century England.

Quite apart from the implications of this for English national life, there are obvious problems attached to the novel's Zionism—not all of them created by hindsight. The novel necessarily puts great emphasis on race and heredity, which effectively allows George Eliot to short-circuit the problems which had preoccupied her throughout her career as a novelist, namely of locating the forces for good in a world of multifarious circumstance. Yet even with this question of the Jews, which seems such a radical departure from her earlier novelistic practice, we can see a familiar pattern at work. As G.H. Lewes wrote to Blackwood, 'I have reflected that [as] she formerly contrived to make one love Methodists, there was no reason why she should not conquer the prejudice against Jews.'[1] In other words, in *Daniel Deronda* George Eliot is engaged yet again on the extension of sympathy: seeking to find a broad ground of common humanity which can unite Jews and Christians, and in doing so overcome those predominantly hostile representations of Jewry which characterise nineteenth-century English culture. The project is carefully plotted in the novel: a series of references to Jews are planted early on, and we are given some strategically placed minor Jewish characters before we come to the section with Mordecai and the discovery of Daniel's Jewishness. Yet, though more ambitious to the extent that prejudice against Jews was much greater than that against Methodists (or Independents or artisans), in essence the problem of gaining the reader's sympathy for Jews remains the same as the problems that marked many of the earlier novels.

One further preoccupation, evident both in *Daniel Deronda* and the earlier novels, will be the main topic of this chapter—the question of the relations between the sexes, and more specifically, what was known in the nineteenth century as 'the Woman Question'. For just as divisions between classes form a central topic in George Eliot's fiction, so too do divisions between the sexes; from the death of Milly Barton in the very first of the *Scenes of Clerical Life* onwards—a scene which demonstrates the redemptive capacities of maternal and feminine affection— we are given a series of representations of women which are both formed by and question the dominant representations of women available in nineteenth-century England. Moreover, not only are gender relations explicitly what many of the novels are 'about', they are equally significant in determing the way the texts are formally organised. So before approaching the question of the way women are presented in the novels, especially in *Daniel Deronda*, we can look at the way gender affects the novel's construction. This question is best approached by asking, what sex is the narrator?

In discussing *Middlemarch*, we saw that there was a wide gap of knowledge between the narrator and the character, the narrator having the concepts and vocabulary to place and explain the characters. This gap was created partly by historical distance and partly by class. Yet it is also, and very importantly, a distance of gender, for the kinds of knowledge that the narrator assumes were, in the nineteenth century especially, male preserves. This fact is represented in *Middlemarch* itself, for one of the reasons why Dorothea makes the mistakes she does, and that she can be so constantly thwarted in her plans, is that she is unable to estimate at their true worth both classical learning and political economy—both 'male' subjects, from which she is excluded as a woman. Yet Dorothea's history is not George Eliot's, who was able to 'master' triumphantly both classical learning, political economy, and a great deal of other knowledge. She was able, in short, to assume an authority deemed masculine in writing her books. Virginia Woolf saw this, but she also saw that this placed George Eliot in a dilemma:

> For her [like her heroines], the burden and complexity of womanhood were not enough; she must reach beyond the sanctuary and pluck for herself the strange bright fruits of art and knowledge. Clasping them as few women have ever clasped them, she would not renounce her own inheritance—the difference of view, the difference of standard—nor accept an inappropriate reward.[2]

To extend Woolf's comment, we can say that on the one hand there is a powerful desire to endorse the idealism and experience of, especially, Maggie Tulliver and Dorothea Brooke; yet equally there is the urge to understand and place their experience. Given the unequal access to knowledge and education in nineteenth-century England, these divergent impulses entail meanings which are determined by gender.

This means, for instance, that the decision to adopt a male pen-name stands out in still bolder relief. In the Introduction I suggested that this decision was largely defensive—an attempt by the atheistical translator of Feuerbach and the scandalous consort of George Henry Lewes, to ward off hostile criticism, and to get the books judged on their merits and not patronised as 'women's writing'. We can now see a further determining impulse: the claim to 'male' authority in matters of knowledge and experience which the narrator makes, would be undermined if the book were known to be written by a woman. Indeed, in *Scenes of Clerical Life* and *Adam Bede* the narrator goes so far as to suggest that he is male; in a similar way Marian Evans, writing her learned reviews and articles for the *Westminster Review*, assumed a male persona. It is a strategy for gaining authority; but the dislocation and disguise involved suggest the repressions and deformations that are forced upon a woman writer in a culture where the right to speak on many issues is decided by being a man.[3]

Well, after *Adam Bede* was published, George Eliot's cover was blown. If thereafter she made no pretence to writing as a man, it remains the case that the narrator of all the novels speaks in the accents of an authority which is partly the authority of male culture. Moreover, George Eliot never permits any of her heroines to storm the bastions of male knowledge in the same way that she herself did; Maggie Tulliver and Dorothea Brooke especially, for whom careers as intellectuals might conceivably have formed escape-routes from an oppressive provincial society, are signally denied the career that Marian Evans managed. This is partly because of a continuing diffidence on George Eliot's part, perhaps even a shrinking dread at the thought of drawing attention to her anomolous social position. Perhaps it was also because George Eliot the realist was determined to find typical solutions to the problems in the novels, and she knew how untypical was her own career. Yet we can also see, in this remarkable absence, the pressure of dominant representations of women for which a career as an intellectual and writer is simply unthinkable.

II

What, then, were these dominant representations? A sentimental poem, by Coventry Patmore, published in 1856, provides a useful shorthand for one dominant representation of the middle-class woman—'The Angel in the House'.[4] In much nineteenth-century English writing, woman's sphere is above all domestic; woman is private, affectionate, emotional, self-sacrificing, deferential. Woman is the end for which man's active public life is the means; woman is the reverent observer of man's greater intellect and larger capacity for action. Various versions of this representation of woman abound in nineteenth-century writing, from sentimental poems like Patmore's to innumerable characters in innumerable novels, and any number of pamphlets, articles, tracts and books. A version of the 'angel in the house' is to be found in the writings of Auguste Comte, propped up by heavy-weight argument. Here woman is to be reverenced as embodying affectionateness, but for this very reason is to be vigorously excluded from any active role in public life. An echo can perhaps even be heard in Virginia Woolf's reference to the 'sanctuary' of womanhood. To what extent does George Eliot's fiction reproduce this dominant and oppressive representation?

The answer, not surprisingly, is a complex one. It is undoubtedly the case that one version of that representation, stressing above all the affectionate and self-sacrificing characteristics of woman, does certainly appear and reappear in the novels. Indeed, given that love and sympathy, which are so important in George Eliot's thinking, are essentially 'feminine' virtues, it is unsurprising that women characters should be the predominant, though by no means the only, bearers of the virtues in the novels. The cohesiveness of human society is ultimately founded on the affections; and 'the mother's yearning is the completest type of the life in another life which is the essence of real human love' (Adam Bede, ch. 43). So, from Dinah Morris through Maggie Tulliver and Romola to Dorothea Brooke, we have a series of characterisations of women who carry the hopes for society's future through their female capacity for affection and renunciation. By the same token, the various critiques of female egoism generally involve women who repudiate their maternal affections and capacity for self-sacrifice; both Hetty Sorrel in Adam Bede and Rosamond in Middlemarch kill their babies (in the latter case, by her carelessness inducing a miscarriage) and refuse to subdue their own desires in favour

115

of others. In *Daniel Deronda* we get the most explicit statement of a view which aligns women with affection, when the narrator draws back from recounting Gwendolen's story to place her in the context of the world-historical American Civil War: 'What in the midst of that mighty drama are girls and their blind visions? They are the Yea or Nay of that good for which men are enduring and fighting. In these delicate vessels is borne onward through the ages the treasure of human affections' (*Daniel Deronda*, ch. 11). It is a Feuerbachian phrase, which reproduces in sophisticated form some elements of the 'angel in the house' as I have described her—girls are 'delicate vessels' who provide a sacred sphere on which human life across the ages is centred. The phrase marks, in fact, one of the limits of George Eliot's representation of women.

Yet this is by no means the last word to be said on the subject. For if the novels do often advance affectionateness, renunciation and self-sacrifice as especially womanly virtues, they are equally committed to a rather different conception of human possibility, in which the gender-specific attributes of affection and intellect are to fuse, or at least be mutually present in the same person, Thus will Ladislaw's striking definition of a poet's soul—'"in which knowledge passes instantaneously into feeling, and feeling flashes back as a new organ of knowledge"' (*Middlemarch*, ch. 22)—can serve as an eloquent indication of what a fully developed human being might be, beyond the reductive definitions which limit men and women to either intellect or affection. Indeed, the attempt to deny women a share in the intellectual culture of the nineteenth century is repeatedly attacked in George Eliot's novels, though perhaps with ultimately ambivalent implications, as we shall see. Here it is worth stressing that reductive definitions of men are equally repudiated with reductive definitions of women. Tom Tulliver, rigid and unfeeling, and Lydgate, emotionally clumsy, are both characterisations which demonstrate the limitations of a male culture which effectively disdains the feminine while simultaneously claiming to reverence it. Daniel Deronda himself can be seen as the sufficient answer to these characterisations; he is both George Eliot's most complete attempt at an unambiguously positive character, and her male hero who shows the greatest capacity for the feminine values of feeling and sympathy.

If one aspect of the 'angel in the house' is that she has an affectionate and self-sacrificing nature, another aspect is her confinement to the private sphere of the home. We are not dealing here simply with an illusion. This representation both colludes with and expresses the real history of middle-class women in the nineteenth century, in their effective exclusion from life outside the home—an exclusion which perhaps increased as the century progressed. Again, we can find evidence in the novels which both supports and subverts this representation of women. If we return once more to *The Mill on the Floss*, it is clear that Tom's character is typically male, while Maggie's is female. This is why Tom can set out to redeem the Tulliver fortunes after the bankruptcy, for as a man he is practical and industrious, and fitted to engage with the world outside the home. Maggie, by contrast, is applauded for confronting the same situation by her heroic renunciation of her own desires—though Philip Wakem's criticism of her behaviour does have a certain force. There is nevertheless an undoubted heroism in her assumption of domestic duties after the pitiful deterioration of her parents. More generally, all of George Eliot's heroines, with the richly ambiguous exception of Maggie herself, end in some form of domestic vocation.

Yet here too we have to record some important countervailing instances to this apparent deference to notions of female confinement. Even the example of Maggie Tulliver requires some modification. She gives a powerful rejoinder to

Philip Wakem when he is pleading with her for a life with 'those who love you': ' "I begin to think there can never come much happiness to me from loving: I have always had so much pain mingled with it. I wish I could make myself a world outside it, as men do" ' (*The Mill on the Floss*, III, 7). Even if it is finally uncertain whether we are to read this wish as yet another desire which Maggie is to renounce, or whether her confinement really does provide an explanation of her frustration and unhappiness, the assertion is powerful enough to threaten complacent views of women's sufficient vocation in the domestic affections.

There are several moments in *Daniel Deronda* also which threaten such views, even though the whole narrative of Gwendolen Harleth might seem to be a prolonged education into the truth that, in Daniel's words, ' "affection is the broadest basis of good in life" ' (*Daniel Deronda*, ch. 35). While Gwendolen's pitiful ignorance about the real obligations of marriage partly explains her disastrous acceptance of Grandcourt, she yet has a comment which, for all its playfulness, does catch some of the power of Maggie's assertion:

> 'We women can't go in search of adventures—to find out the North-West Passage or the source of the Nile, or to hunt tigers in the East. We must stay where we grow, or where the gardeners like to transplant us. We are brought up like the flowers, to look as pretty as we can, and be dull without complaining. That is my notion about the plants; they are often bored, and that is the reason why some of them have got poisonous.' (*Daniel Deronda*, ch. 13)

Even if we make full allowance for the irony which works against Gwendolen—she is talking for effect, and we also know that one of her handicaps is that she has been so often 'transplanted' that her moral life has had no chance to root itself in a loved locality—even if we make these allowances there remains a hard core of genuine protest against the circumscribed possibilities that limit a woman's life.

Two further instances in the novel work strongly against the notions that women ought to be confined to the home or that they are peculiarly fitted to renunciation and self-sacrifice. The first comes with the irruption into the novel of Daniel's mother when she decides to tell him of his parentage. The Princess Halm-Eberstein, once the celebrated opera singer the Alcharisi, has some very powerful rhetoric to justify her decision to break out of the constraints of Judaism to pursue her career on the stage. She denies to Daniel that he can imagine the hardship of being asked to renounce that ambition:

> 'No.... You are not a woman. You may try—but you can never imagine what it is to have a man's force of genius in you, and yet to suffer the slavery of being a girl. To have a pattern cut out—"this is the Jewish woman; this is what you must be; this is what you are wanted for; a woman's heart must be of such a size and no larger, else it must be pressed small, like Chinese feet; her happiness is to be made as cakes are, by a fixed receipt." That was what my father wanted. He wished I had been a son, he cared for me as a make-shift link.' (*Daniel Deronda*, ch. 51)

What is so interesting about this rhetoric is that it works against some of the most cherished ostensible meanings of the novel. The Princess explicitly and powerfully asserts the right of the individual to construct a meaningful life independently of the wider continuities of race or the higher responsibilities of womanhood, when elsewhere the novel is concerned to discover and endorse them. Moreover, Daniel himself, one of principal articulators of these higher truths, is brought by the Alcharisi to acknowledge her right to self-assertion, at least as far as her artistic career is concerned. When she says, ' "My nature gave me a charter" ' (*Daniel Deronda*, ch. 53), Daniel agrees. It is perhaps possible to use this phrase as a way of

119

reincorporating the Alcharisi back into agreement with the dominant meanings of the text: she is an exception, a woman so unusually gifted as to afford no example. Yet the force of her rhetoric remains to disturb the ostensible commitment of the novel to submission to the duties of maternity and the solidarity of race.

Another similar moment which tends to contradict the ostensible meaning of the novel occurs towards the end of the book, and it works against the authority of Mordecai—the only occasion when his prophetic role appears oppressive. At this point in the story Mirah is in love with Daniel, but is suffering because she mistakenly imagines that Daniel is in love with Gwendolen. Mordecai is ignorant of this, and insists upon telling her that as a woman she is particularly able to understand his own joy in renunciation:

'And yet,' said Mordecai, rather insistently, 'women are specially framed for the love which feels possession in renouncing, and is thus a fit image of what I mean. Somewhere in the later *Midrash*, I think, is the story of a Jewish maiden who loved a Gentile king so well, that this was what she did: she entered into prison and changed clothes with the woman who was beloved by the king, that she might deliver that woman from death by dying in her stead, and leave the king to be happy in his love which was not for her. This is the surpassing love, that loses self in the object of love.'

'No, Ezra, no,' said Mirah, with low-toned intensity, 'that was not it. She wanted the king when she was dead to know what she had done, and feel that she was better than the other. It was her strong self, wanting to conquer, that made her die.'. . .

'My sister, thou hast read too many plays, where the writers delight in showing the human passions as indwelling demons, unmixed with the relenting and devout elements of the soul. Thou judgest by the plays, and not by thy own heart, which is like our mother's.'

Mirah made no answer. (*Daniel Deronda*, ch. 61)

This is an extremely significant exchange, and a very moving one. A tremendous weight of repressed desire is weighing upon the speech of both Mordecai and Mirah here, with Mirah's final silence signifying her eventual distressed submission to her own loss—though equally it signifies her refusal to accept Mordecai's insistence upon her pleasure in such renunciation. In addition, her alternative interpretation of the woman's story from the *Midrash* is powerful and unexpected; for under the pressure of her own desire she exposes an exemplary story of woman's renunciation as a story of jealousy, revenge and self-assertion. As such, the incident perhaps enables us to look more sceptically at those other exemplary renunciations in George Eliot's writing, such as Maggie Tulliver's or Dorothea Brooke's; we can ask what repressed desires for 'conquest' are being managed in their moments of submission. The scene certainly enables us to see the unassuaged pain that remains in the act of renunciation, and invites us to question the too insistent male belief in the love that 'feels possession in renouncing'.

So what are we to make of these various examples, which work against a dominant and oppressive representation of woman, to which some countenance is ostensibly given elsewhere in the novels? What general description of the novel can we give which takes account of these ambiguities and potential contradictions? It is not sufficient to rest in ambiguity, though some support can be found for such a view in George Eliot's letters, when she wrote that 'there is no subject on which I am more inclined to hold my peace and learn, than on the "Woman Question". It seems to me to overhang abysses, of which even prostitution is not the worst.'[5] If we simply say that different incidents, characterisation and comments in the novels point in different directions we ignore the evident labour on George Eliot's part to sort them into coherence and consistency. It is much more helpful to revert to the notion of a 'discursive hierarchy' which I advanced as characteristic of the realist novel.

In the terms of this description, such a novel is made up of a variety of different discourses, which are sorted into a hierarchy by the authoritative or 'master' discourse which has the capacity to explain and place the discourse beneath it. Since the different discourses that a novel combines are socially produced and have their own histories, they are likely to represent the world in different ways, and draw on different ideological resources. The Alcharisi's speech, for example, gives powerful expression to a kind of liberalism which pits the individual against oppressive social constraints, so that the rhetoric draws its strength from different notions to those that are advanced elsewhere in the novel. What we must now add to this notion of a discursive hierarchy is the recognition that its various discourses are charged with the strength of people's wishes, ambitions and desires. To that extent we should perhaps replace the notion of a hierarchy by the notion of an economy; any novel sets in play a variety of different impulses and desires through and across its different discourses, whose ultimate value can only be assessed when the novel reaches a conclusion. Moreover, it is an unstable economy, as the example of both *The Mill on the Floss* and *Daniel Deronda* suggest. While the former novel ostensibly seeks to endorse female renunciation and self-sacrifice, the value that actually attaches to Maggie's desire, or her powerful assertion of the need to make a world 'outside love', is liable to overturn the careful constructions designed to contain it. Similarly in *Daniel Deronda*, the various instances that I have noted, of the Alcharisi, of Mirah's scepticism of her brother, and of Gwendolen's very attractiveness, all tend to upset the economy of the novel which seeks to assign them a diminished value.

So these various examples, which draw on different ideological resources from the ostensible meanings of the novel and thus work against these meanings, cannot easily be integrated into a coherent, integrated or organic view of the novel. Novels are not naturally organic; there is considerable labour involved in smoothing out contradictions or inconsistencies between the various discourses that any novel combines. It need not be one's responsibility as a reader to help this labour along by assuming, in the case of seeming contradiction, that the truth must fall flatly between two differing assertions in an unstated compromise; or alternatively to view the whole novel as containing a complex yet resolved ambiguity. As far as *Daniel Deronda* is concerned, we have noted various instances which disrupt the coherence of the text. The point is not to celebrate these disruptive moments; but neither is it to George Eliot's discredit that we recognise them. For they testify to the ambition and self-confidence of her belief that she can manage the economy of the novel to contain them.

III

George Eliot's novels, then, are governed by an economy which in part seeks to contain women's desires as they are addressed to the satisfaction of their own wills. It is important to add, of course, that this is a general lesson that the novels seek to inculcate: men as much as women have to learn the importance of submission and renunciation in the face of duty or where the happiness of others is affected. Yet given the intensely affectionate nature of the women characters as she conceives them, submission and self-sacrifice tend to press especially hard upon them in George Eliot's novels. To that extent the novels are deeply antipathetic to one version of feminism as it has been articulated over the last 150 years. In this version, whose ideological resources, like the Alcharisi's, are essentially liberal, the point of feminism is to extend to women the same rights to self-fulfilment as are already enjoyed by men as 'free agents'. Liberalism essentially defines liberty as doing what one likes. For George Eliot, however, true liberty is submission to a higher law. Thus in *Daniel Deronda*, it is Gwendolen's continuing mistake to imagine that her happiness will consist in having 'empire' or control over her own life. Quite the contrary, her happiness, if it is imaginable at all at the end of the novel, will depend on her ability to align her life with wider responsiblities and duties, so that she might see her brief life, in the solemn words of the 'Proem' to *Romola*, as 'an arc in an immeasurable circle of light and glory'.

The 'Woman Question', therefore, as so often in George Eliot's writing, tends to resolve itself into a question of knowledge. How can one ensure that women can know or become conscious of that higher law or that wider responsibility which is the condition, if not of happiness, at least of a meaningful life? It is thus entirely consistent that George Eliot should have supported one central demand of nineteenth-century feminism, for equality in education for women. For the point of education, in this view, is to lead to a recognition of the fundamental or underlying conditions of human life; in short, the laws that govern it. If women are kept in ignorance of these laws, not only are they likely to be unfitted for their sacred trust of caring for young children, they are also likely to be locked into triviality and egoism. Throughout the novels, egoism for women tends to mean the substitution of trivial and socially ambitious desires for the more fundamental knowledge which can measure such ambitions and reject them in favour of the demands of sympathy and affection. What is wrong with women's education, and indeed with men's expectations of women, is that it only fits woman to be an ornament when it should be fitting her to be a helpmate.

You might not think that this is a very radical position, but it is nevertheless capable of generating a powerful critique of women's education. The most striking and extended study of the results of inadequate education is Rosamond Vincy in *Middlemarch*, 'a sylph caught young and educated at Mrs Lemon's' (*Middlemarch*, ch. 16). Her education is in effect a list of 'accomplishments', designed only to make her attractive in the marriage market, and quite unfitting her for life after marriage. She is thus disabled from appreciating the nobility of Lydgate's medical ambitions, and substitutes instead the ambitions of rank and elegant leisure. However, it is not only Rosamond's unfitness as a wife for Lydgate that is so damning in its implications for her education, for perhaps the most telling aspect of the characterisation is her self-consciousness. By keeping her in ignorance of those forces which really make life worthwhile, her education (and indeed her general position as the belle of Middlemarch) has left her prey to a profound inauthenticity. Everything she does and every pose she adopts is done for effect, and calculated to display her to advantage:

> (Every nerve and muscle in Rosamond was adjusted to the consciousness that she was being looked at. She was by nature an actress of parts that entered into her *physique*: she even acted her own character, and so well, that she did not know it to be precisely her own.) (*Middlemarch*, ch. 12)

This kind of inauthenticity means that her own life has effectively been robbed from her.

Though very different, and ultimately redeemed, Gwendolen Harleth is another study of the inadequacy of women's education. She is indeed, as the title of Book 1 indicates, 'The Spoiled Child'. However, as with Rosamond Vincy, it is not sufficient just to label this 'egoism' and pass on, for, as again with Rosamond, Gwendolen too is not responsible for her own irresponsiblity. We are given in *Daniel Deronda* an extensive study of a milieu and a culture which inculcates false ideals of worth and yet also makes it impossible for women to achieve even those ideals. Consider, for example, the following dialogue between Gwendolen and her first ingenuous suitor, Rex Gascoigne; some of it of course anticipates her later conversation with Grandcourt that I have already quoted. Gwendolen begins:

'Girls' lives are so stupid: they never do what they like.'
'I thought that was more the case of the men. They are forced to do hard things, and are often dreadfully bored, and knocked to pieces too. And then, if we love a girl very dearly, we want to do as she likes, so after all you have your own way.'
'I don't believe it. I never saw a married woman who had her own way.'
'What should you like to do?' said Rex, quite guilelessly, and in real anxiety.
'Oh, I don't know!—go to the North Pole, or ride steeplechases, or go to be a queen in the East like Lady Hester Stanhope,' said Gwendolen, flightily. Her words were born on her lips, but she would have been at a loss to give an answer of deeper origin. (*Daniel Deronda*, ch. 7)

It is a superb piece of dialogue, in part because the ironies are so difficult to disentangle: the exchange is a mixture of naivety, frustration, false sophistication, legitimate discontent, and misconceived ambition. Gwendolen's inability to formulate any less flighty ideal—or perhaps one should say, more realistic ideal—is a direct product of a culture which defines happiness as doing what one likes: this is one sense in which she has been spoiled. Yet it is also true that girls' lives are indeed stupid in this society; we are given a series of telling instances of the genteel stupidity which besets the lives of women whose only ambition can be to win a husband.

So Gwendolen's tragedy—if, indeed, it is one—is that she fails to see beyond the arid perspective of a culture that defines happiness as doing what one likes, or for display. In this, we are explicitly invited to view her as an object of pity—'poor Gwendolen had never dissociated happiness from personal pre-eminence and eclat' (*Daniel Deronda*, ch. 24). So while it is true that under the pressure of hard circumstance she does repudiate the claims represented by Lydia Glasher when she marries Grandcourt, it is equally the case that she is under the most colossal misapprehension about what marriage entails. Throughout she entertains 'the reassuring thought that marriage would be the gate into a larger freedom' (ch. 14), still believing on the verge of her marriage that, 'What could not a woman do when she was married, if she knew how to assert herself?' On this illusion the text is explicit: 'Here all was constructive imagination. Gwendolen had about as accurate a conception of marriage— that is to say, of the mutual influences, demands, duties of man and woman in the state of matrimony—as she had of magnetic currents and the law of storms' (ch. 27). Gwendolen, in short, is as much a victim of a vicious education as she is responsible for her wrong-doing.

But this is not the only way in which the dice are loaded against her. Let us say that official culture is represented by Mr Gascoigne, who likes to temper his worldliness with a little sentiment. He advises Gwendolen to accept Grandcourt but does not like it that she should do so for worldly reasons: 'He wished his niece parks, carriages, a title—everything that would make this world a pleasant abode; but he wished her not to be cynical—to be, on the contrary, religiously dutiful, and have warm domestic affections' (*Daniel Deronda*, ch. 13). This is the kind of oppressive double-bind that Gwendolen partly sees through. There is, however, a much more oppressive aspect of this culture of which she is necessarily ignorant: that exclusively male and thoroughly sexist sub-culture in which women are assessed, gossip about mistresses exchanged, sexual exploits boasted of. We see here one of the advantages of the narrator's access to male knowledge and experience, for it enables him/her to make fully accessible to the reader the forces which are acting on Gwendolen but of which she herself cannot know. One such pressure is her very success in terms of this sub-culture, which effectively makes her a desirable status symbol. Thus when she is at the archery meeting she is being shown off as a possible wife for the assembled onlookers:

> 'That girl is like a high-mettled racer,' said Lord Brackenshaw to young Clintock, one of the invited spectators.
>
> 'First chop! tremendously pretty, too,' said the elegant Grecian, who had been paying her assiduous attention; 'I never saw her look better.' (*Daniel Deronda*, ch. 10)

To describe the second speaker here as the 'elegant Grecian' neatly spears the double standards of male culture, for the operative judgement on a woman is here made in aristocratic slang quite at odds with the classical culture to which a 'Grecian' (i.e. a classical scholar) is officially committed. Moreover, the description of Gwendolen as a 'high-mettled racer' is the first of a series of descriptions of her as a thoroughbred horse who has to be 'mastered'—Grandcourt, for example, exults after she has accepted him that she has been 'brought to kneel down like a horse under training for the arena, though she might have an objection to it all the while' (*Daniel Deronda*, ch. 28). This offensive image, a subliminally sexual one, carries the effective valuation of this society and Gwendolen cannot but be ignorant of it.

Indeed, it is Grandcourt's knowledge of and success in this unofficial male sub-culture which is part of his benumbing power over Gwendolen after their marriage. If Gwendolen is innocent of any knowledge that could put her duties and responsibilities in a wider context, she is equally ignorant of that masculine knowledge of the world which, to recall Mr Christian's phrase from *Felix Holt*, 'knew the price-current of most things' (*Felix Holt*, ch. 36). Grandcourt has the power to confine Gwendolen because he too has such a knowledge: ' "What do *you* know about the world? You have married me, and must be guided by my opinion" ' (*Daniel Deronda*, ch. 48); and Gwendolen of course lacks that wider knowledge which could truly reckon this 'opinion'. ' "The higher life must be a region in which the affections are clad with knowledge" ' (*Daniel Deronda*, ch. 36), Daniel tells Gwendolen; her difficulty in the novel is to struggle through to that higher life and both the affections and knowledge which characterise it.

While nominally deferential to this higher life, like Mr Gascoigne with his talk of religious duty and the warm domestic affections, society as it is represented in *Daniel Deronda* effectively ignores it. George Eliot takes some pains to expose the ways that effective evaluations, especially men's since they are the most powerful people in the novel, differ from the ostensible valuations. The contrast between two typical assertions of Grandcourt sufficiently makes the point. The first is to Gwendolen while he is still courting her; it represents a kind of gallantry: ' "How you treat us poor devils of men! . . . we are always getting the worst of it" ' (*Daniel Deronda*, ch. 29). In the following chapter, in speaking to his mistress Lydia Glasher who has now become an encumbrance to him, the tone of badinage has been replaced by his effective judgement: ' "Infernal idiots that women are!" ' (*Daniel Deronda*, ch. 30). This is not merely an example of Grandcourt's refusal to accept responsibility for or commitment to Lydia Glasher; the contrast is symptomatic of a rift in male culture. This rift is most exposed by the story of Lydia Glasher.

Gwendolen marries Grandcourt in the full knowledge that he has been supporting a mistress and family for several years. In itself this might be thought to represent a rather abstract kind of wrong-doing on Gwendolen's part; throughout her career as a novelist, after all, George Eliot has insisted on the necessity for familiarity and multiple association as the basis for moral obligation. Yet the revelation that Grandcourt has a mistress deeply shocks Gwendolen, and we are clearly to understand it to be a great wrong on her part to marry Grandcourt in spite of this knowledge. Why should this be so?

Let us recall the scene when Gwendolen is confronted by Lydia, at the Whispering Stones, with Gwendolen on the verge of accepting Grandcourt: 'Gwendolen, watching Mrs Glasher's face as she spoke, felt a sort of terror: it was as if some ghastly vision had come to her in a dream and said, "I am a woman's life"' (*Daniel Deronda*, ch. 14). The 'ghastly vision' recalls the death's head behind the panel at Offendene which so frightened Gwendolen as she was posing as Hermione. Mrs Glasher's appearance is thus connected with the final responsibilities and limits of humanity which necessarily appear terrifying if you attempt habitually to exclude them. In one sense, therefore, it is against this consciousness and this responsibility that Gwendolen offends by ignoring Lydia's greater claim on Grandcourt, and it is for this reason that her experience at the Whispering Stones induces in her a sense of meaninglessness in life: Gwendolen 'brought from her late experience a vague impression that in this confused world it signified nothing what anyone did, so that they amused themselves' (*Daniel Deronda*, ch. 15). Yet it is obviously equally important that the vision should seem to say 'I am a *woman's* life'. For the appearance of Lydia Glasher initiates Gwendolen into the effective behaviour and valuations of men towards women; the meeting lifts the veil of decency which obscures the double-standard. The promise that Lydia exacts from Gwendolen, not to marry Grandcourt, springs from an instinctive female solidarity which is the only defence against the double standard; it is against this solidarity that Gwendolen offends when she breaks the promise. The scene takes on a fearful representativeness for

Gwendolen because Lydia's fate combines her own sense of powerlessness with this initiation into men's effective behaviour; yet thanks to her very innocence she does not have the capacity fully to come to terms with or understand the significance of the revelation.

So, while Gwendolen is certainly wilful, she is also caught in a series of double-binds which are not of her own making. She is the victim of a culture which officially defers to sentiment but in practice values material comfort. She acts on a belief that happiness consists in the exercise of her will, only to find herself in a marriage which is a battle of wills that she is bound to lose as a woman. And she is the unknowing victim of an aristocratic male culture in which a woman's sexual attractiveness counts in a system of competitive display: 'It was to be supposed of [Grandcourt] that he would put up with nothing less that the best in outward equipment, wife included; and the bride was what he might have been expected to choose' (*Daniel Deronda*, ch. 35). This damning comment captures both Grandcourt's own valuation of Gwendolen and the valuation of a society—it is part of a general expectation to equate a wife with 'outward equipment'. The complex and mutually interlocking ironies generated from these various false valuations and mis-apprehensions make the texture of the novel in those scenes which deal with Gwendolen especially self-sufficient and difficult to penetrate or situate.

We can nevertheless ask by what standards we are to judge this behaviour and the valuations that accompany it. Where is the authoritative discourse which can place Mr Gascoigne's worldliness or Grandcourt's aristocratic drawl? For the presence of such a discourse is sufficiently indicated by the irony which surround the phrase like 'the best in outward equipment, wife included'. Unlike *Middlemarch*, *Daniel Deronda* relies much less on commentary to place the various discourses of the story. Rather, the authority in the book is shared between a comparatively discreet commentary and two discourses internal to the story, the speech of Daniel and the prophetic utterance of Mordecai. In the context of this chapter we can notice two related points. First, the irony that works against the various discourses in which Gwendolen is enmeshed is especially directed against certain key words like 'empire', 'mastery' and 'pre-eminence'. Secondly, Daniel brings a language of affection and sympathy to bear upon Gwendolen's case. With both these points in mind we can see that male values are being measured and tested by female ones. Although the accents of authority in this novel are in part male, they nevertheless speak meanings that are implicitly female.

So we can now gloss more fully Virginia Woolf's comment that George Eliot would not 'renounce her own inheritance— the difference of view, the difference of standard'. There is a dual impulse in the novels, to attain the right to speak arrogated by men, and yet to retain the inheritance of affection and solidarity that is a defence against that arrogation. We can see in George Eliot's writing, in other words, though worked through according to her own logic, a version of that dilemma which faced nineteenth-century feminism. How can women fight for a place in a man's world without losing those qualities of mutual support and affection? Or to put this the other way round, if women value especially those qualities of affection and solidarity, isn't this to defer to reductive male definitions which marginalise women and exclude them from the real business of the world? George Eliot worked through this dilemma by stressing women's affectionateness and capacity for renunciation. Nevertheless she could use these values to mount an attack on a world made sterile in part by male values of empire and competitiveness. Paradoxically, in fact, she used a conservative definition of femininity to mount a radical attack on the world. Different forms of this paradox have marked the history of feminism, and indeed remain with us to this day.[6]

132

Conclusion

Henry James, who had rather mixed feelings about George Eliot's later work, concluded a review of *Middlemarch* in this way: 'It sets a limit, we think, to the development of the old-fashioned English novel. Its diffuseness . . . makes it too copious a dose of pure fiction. If we write novels so, how shall we write History?'[1] Whether or not we agree that George Eliot's writing is too diffuse to be enjoyable as pure fiction, the comment does bring into sharp focus one of the main concerns of this book, with respect to all of George Eliot's novels and not just *Middlemarch*. For her writing does indeed represent the most ambitious and the best sustained attempt in fiction to understand and explain the whole movement of a society, in terms which are rational, flexible and secular.

In the course of this book I have suggested some of the tensions and ambiguities involved in this project. George Eliot's realism, we saw, is directed towards the extension of the reader's sympathies, towards finding a ground of common humanity that will bind reader, writer and character together in a moral solidarity that should transcend the accidents of class, race or historical situation. Her aesthetic, in short, is assimilative and integrative. If we ask how we are to locate and understand her writing historically, we must place this aesthetic as part of a wider middle-class attempt to ground and legitimise their rule of society.

Yet George Eliot's writing has survived the moment of its inception. Looking back at this body of writing after the passage of over a hundred years, are there aspects of it which are still live and valuable? Certainly it costs us little now, as readers of these novels, to extend our sympathies to their various characters and the wider groups of people they represent. Neither does it cost us much to find grounds for sympathy with those characters with whom George Eliot herself found it most difficult to sympathise, like Hetty Sorrel in *Adam Bede*, or the inhabitants of the steward's room of Treby Manor in *Felix Holt*, or Rosamond Vincy in *Middlemarch*. The problems really begin when we ask, in the very different conditions of today, where that commitment to sympathy takes us now. Given the extraordinarily varied means of knowledge and communication that surround us, the results of such an inquiry might still be surprising and even disturbing.

But perhaps George Eliot's real challenge remains her emphasis upon understanding. No one now believes in the 'positive synthesis', or subscribes to any of the particular intellectual positions which she sought to promote in her novels. Yet the project upon which she was engaged remains as urgent as ever: in the most general terms, people must still seek to understand themselves and their past if they wish to intervene successfully in the present. In George Eliot's own words, 'it would be a very serious mistake to suppose that the study of the past and the labours of criticism have no important practical bearing on the present.'[2] This was true of George Eliot's own study of the past. Our own very different 'labours of criticism', in seeking to understand our own past which now includes George Eliot, can and ought to assert the very possibility of understanding to which her whole work bears such powerful testimony.

Notes

Introduction

1 Virginia Woolf, 'General Eliot', in *A Century of George Eliot Criticism*, ed. G.S. Haight (Houghton Mifflin, Boston, Mass., 1965), p. 187.
2 For a brief account of this tendentious opposition between 'realist' and 'modernist' writing, see F. Jameson, *The Political Unconscious* (1981), pp. 17–18.

Chapter 1

1 Ludwig Feuerbach, *The Essence of Christianity*, trans. Marian. Evans (3rd edn, London 1893), p. 271.
2 *Ibid.*, p. vii.
3 *Ibid.*, p. 9.
4 G.H. Lewes, *Comte's Philosophy of the Sciences* (London, 1853), p. 1.
5 George Eliot, 'Address to Working Men by Felix Holt', Appendix A to *Felix Holt, the Radical*, ed. and intro. Peter Coveney (Penguin, Harmondsworth, 1972), p. 626.
6 'Auguste Comte and Positivism', in *The Essential Writings*, ed.

Gertrude Lenzer (Harper & Row, New York and London, 1975), p. 400.
7   Quoted in G.S. Haight, *George Eliot, A Biography* (Clarendon Press, Oxford, 1968), pp. 219–20.

Chapter 2

1   'The Natural History of German Life', in *Essays of George Eliot*, ed. Thomas Pinney (Columbia University Press, New York/Routledge & Kegan Paul, London, 1963), pp. 170–1.
2   See above, p. 23.
3   Raymond Williams, *Keywords* (Flamingo, 1983).
4   This point is forcefully made by David Lodge in his Introduction to *Scenes of Clerical Life*, ed. David Lodge (Penguin, Harmondsworth, 1973).
5   William Blake, 'The Human Abstract', in *Songs of Experience* (1794).

Chapter 3

1   The George Eliot Letters, ed. G.S. Haight, 9 vols (Yale University Press, New Haven and London, 1954–78) IV, 49. Hereafter cited as *Letters*.
2   'Servants' Logic', in *Essays of George Eliot*.
3   *Letters*, III, 474.
4   *Ibid.*, IV, 97.
5   J.B. Bullen, 'George Eliot's *Romola* as a Positivist Allegory', *Review of English Studies*, 26 (1975), 425–35.
6   W.F.T. Myers, 'George Eliot: Politics and Personality', in *Literature and Politics in the Nineteenth Century*, ed. John Lucas (Methuen, London, 1975), pp. 105–29.

Chapter 4

1   The point is made in passing by George Levine, 'George Eliot's Hypothesis of Reality', *Nineteenth-Century Fiction*, 35 (1980–81), 1–28.

2 F.R. Leavis, *The Great Tradition* (Chatto & Windus, London, 1947). D. Daiches, in *George Eliot: Middlemarch* (Arnold, London, 1963), provides the most complete ironic account of Dorothea.
3 Sidney Colvin, *Fortnightly Review*, 13 (19 January 1873), 142–7. Available in David Carroll, *George Eliot: The Critical Heritage* (Routledge & Kegan Paul, London, 1971), pp. 331–8.
4 Compare her note on the 'historic imagination' in 'Leaves from a Note-book', in *Essays of George Eliot*: 'by veracious imagination, I mean the working out in detail of the various steps by which a political or social change was reached, using all extant evidence and supplying deficiencies by careful analogical creation', p.446.
5 For an account of *Middlemarch* as a discursive hierarchy in a much more hostile manner, see Colin MacCabe, *James Joyce and the Revolution of the Word* (Macmillan, London, 1979).
6 The 'showing/telling' distinction, which has a long history, is delicately expressed in Henry James' prefaces to his novels, ed. R.P. Blackmur as *The Art of the Novel* (Scribner, New York, 1948). The distinction was given normative authority by Percy Lubbock in *The Craft of Fiction* (London, 1921), and by any number of subsequent Anglo-American critics. Colin MacCabe's hostility to George Eliot on anti-realist, postmodernist grounds, is a distant descendant of these early modernist positions.

Chapter 5

1 *Letters*, VI, 196.
2 Virginia Woolf, 'George Eliot', in *A Century of George Eliot Criticism*, p. 189.
3 The ambiguous nature of George Eliot's authority, both as internal narrator and for her literary 'daughters', is discussed by Sandra M. Gilbert, in 'Life's Empty Pack: Notes towards a Literary Daughteronomy', *Critical Inquiry*, 11 (1985), 355–84.
4 Coventry Patmore, *The Angel in the House* (1856).
5 *Letters*, V, 58.
6 In her pioneering synoptic history of feminism, *Faces of Feminism* (1981), Olive Banks argues that, as the nineteenth century progressed, the tradition of feminism, descended from

Evangelicalism and which stressed female difference and moral superiority, increasingly dominated an alternative 'equal rights' tradition descended from the Enlightenment. The tensions and ambiguities of George Eliot's representations of women that I have described in this chapter perhaps derive from her adherence to that first tradition, which shared many of the discursive terms of the anti-feminism which opposed it.

Conclusion

1   Henry James, *Galaxy* (March 1873), xv, 424–28, in *The Critical Heritage*, p. 359.
2   'The Progress of the Intellect', in *Essays of George Eliot*, p. 28.

Chronology of the Life of George Eliot

1806   Robert Evans, father of George Eliot, moves to South Farm near Nuneaton, Warwickshire, as agent of Francis Newdigate of Arbury Hall, Warwickshire.

1819   22 November. Birth of Mary Anne Evans (GE) at South Farm.

1820   The Evans family move to Griff House, Chilvers Coton, near Nuneaton.

1828   GE sent to boarding school in Nuneaton, where she comes under influence of Maria Lewis, an Evangelical teacher.

1830–32 Reform crisis culminates in the passage of the Reform Act 1832.

1832   GE becomes a pupil at the Miss Franklins' School Coventry.

1835   GE starts to keep house for her father at Griff.

1841   GE moves with her father to Foleshill, Coventry. She makes the acquaintance of the Brays and the Hennells.

1842   GE abandons orthodox Christianity.

1846   Publication of GE's translation of D.F. Strauss's *The Life of Jesus, Critically Examined.*

1848   Year of Revolutions. GE enthusiastic about the first French uprising in February.

1849   30 May, death of Robert Evans.

1849–50 GE in Geneva, recovering from her father's death and deciding on a future career.

1851–57 Intellectual life in London. Effective editor of *Westminster Review* for John Chapman. Meets Herbert Spencer. Many articles and reviews published in *Westminster Review*, the *Leader*, etc. 20 July 1854 GE leaves England for Weimar in the company of George Henry Lewes, a union which will last until his death.

1854   July, publication of GE's translation of Feuerbach's *The Essence of Christianity.*

1857   *Scenes of Clerical Life* published anonymously in *Blackwood's Magazine.* Blackwood to be GE's publisher for all her subsequent books except *Romola.* May, GE informs her older brother about her 'marriage' to G.H. Lewes; Isaac Evans refuses any further communication with her.

1859   *Adam Bede* published under the pseudonym George Eliot. The book is a tremendous success.

1860–63 GE and Lewes live at 16 Blandford Square, London.

1860   *The Mill on the Floss.*

1861   *Silas Marner.*

1863   *Romola* published in the *Cornhill Magazine.*

1863–78 GE and Lewes live at The Priory, Regent's Park, London. Despite their anomalous social position, they gradually win acceptance from 'society'; they have regular intellectual receptions on Sunday afternoons.

1866	*Felix Holt, the Radical.*
1867	Second Reform Act.
1868	*The Spanish Gypsy*, an epic poem, published after a long visit to Spain.
1870–71	Franco-Prussian war powerfully revives GE's interest in contemporary social and political affairs.
1871–72	*Middlemarch* published in eight books.
1876	*Daniel Deronda* published in a similar format.
1877	GE and Lewes acquire Witley Heights in Surrey; the acquisition of a country house marks the final stage in their progress to respectability.
1878	30 November, George Henry Lewes dies.
1879	*Impressions of Theophrastus Such*, a series of essays in the tradition of Lamb's *Essays of Elia* or Thackeray's *Roundabout Papers*.
1880	6 May, GE marries John Walter Cross, banker. 22 December, GE dies.

Suggestions for Further Reading

A book of this kind is especially reliant on the work of other critics and scholars, most of whom are not mentioned in the following, very compressed list. I hope you will find it useful if you wish to follow up any of the ideas and suggestions of the book, though it is probably the case that most of the suggestions will only be available in a university library or equivalent.

George Eliot's Life

The George Eliot Letters, ed. G. S. Haight, 9 vols (Yale University Press, New Haven and London, 1954–78). Obviously you won't want to read all nine volumes! However, the edition is very well indexed and it is often worthwhile and enjoyable to pursue a particular line of inquiry through the index.

G. S. Haight, *George Eliot: A Biography* (Oxford University Press, New York and Oxford, 1968). This is the most complete modern biography, enjoyable to read if not especially adventurous.

The Intellectual Context

Essays of George Eliot, ed. T. Pinney (Columbia University Press, New York/Routledge & Kegan Paul, London, 1963). Indispensable.

Auguste Comte, *The Essential Writings*, ed. Gertrud Leuzer (Harper & Row, New York and London, 1975). Even this highly abridged edition gives you more Comte than you will want to read, but there is an excellent introduction by the editor.

Ludwig Feuerbach, *The Essence of Christianity*, trans. Marian Evans (London, 3rd edn, 1893). If you can persist with the unfamiliar idiom of German philosophy, this can be an enjoyable and exciting book to read.

J. W. Burrow, *Evolution and Society* (Cambridge University Press, London, 1966). Though not principally about George Eliot, Burrow gives here an excellent account of her intellectual tradition.

Criticism of George Eliot

George Eliot: The Critical Heritage, ed. David Carroll (Routledge & Kegan Paul, London 1971). Provides a very useful collection of criticism by George Eliot's contemporaries.

A Century of George Eliot Criticism, ed. G. S. Haight (Houghton Mifflin, Boston, Mass., 1965). A convenient way of getting some sense of the history of George Eliot's reputation, with some of the key essays by Henry James, Leslie Stephen and Virginia Woolf.

Critical Essays on George Eliot, ed. Barbara Hardy (Routledge & Kegan Paul, London, 1979). See especially the essays by John Goode on *Adam Bede* and Graham Martin on *Daniel Deronda*.

George Eliot: Centenary Essays and an Unpublished Fragment, ed. Anne Smith (Vision, London 1980). See especially the essay by Graham Martin on *The Mill on the Floss* and by

Susan Meikle on *Middlemarch*.

W. F. T. Myers, *The Teaching of George Eliot* (Leicester University Press, Leicester, 1984). This provides both the fullest account of George Eliot as a Positivist, as well as a powerful modern assessment of this whole intellectual tradition.

W. F. T. Myers, 'George Eliot: Politics and Personality', in *Literature and Politics in the Nineteenth Century*, ed. John Lucas (Methuen, London, 1975), pp. 105-29. Suggestive account of George Eliot's rejection of politics, narrowly conceived, with particular relevance to *Felix Holt*.

George Levine, 'George Eliot's Hypothesis of Reality', *Nineteenth-Century Fiction*, 35 (1980-81), 1-28. Brilliantly uses nineteenth-century theories of scientific discovery (especially that of George Henry Lewes) to suggest ways in which George Eliot's notion of realism changed through her career; especially useful for *Daniel Deronda*.

Joseph Butwin, 'The Pacification of the Crowd: From "Janet's Repentance" to *Felix Holt*', *Nineteenth-Century Fiction*, 35 (1980-81), 349-71. A witty and informative essay on some of the central tensions and ambiguities of George Eliot's writing.

Catherine Gallagher, 'The Failure of Realism: *Felix Holt*', *Nineteenth-Century Fiction*, 35 (1980-81), 372-84. Usefully locates some of the difficulties of *Felix Holt* in the crisis of liberalism in the 1860s.

Criticism: General

Raymond Williams, *The English Novel from Dickens to Lawrence* (Chatto & Windus, London, 1970). This reverses the usual order of critical judgement by placing George Eliot's early work over the later; Williams does so in the context both of an argument about her as an intellectual and of a wider argument about the development of the English novel. Accessible and important.

Terry Eagleton, *Criticism and Ideology* (NLB, London, 1976). A difficult book by the foremost English Marxist critic, it nevertheless contains a brilliant series of thumbnail sketches of nineteenth- and twentieth-century novelists, including George Eliot.

Sandra M. Gilbert and Susan Gubar, *The Madwoman in the Attic: The Woman Writer and the Nineteenth Century Literary Imagination* (Yale University Press, New Haven, 1979). A pioneering piece of feminist criticism. Rather uneven, but occasionally very exciting.

Shlomith Rimmon-Kenan, *Narrative Fiction: Contemporary Poetics*, (Methuen, London and New York, 1983). A compact handbook of formal analysis of narrative, which would be useful if you want to pursue the distinction between commentary and story, or the notion of a discursive hierarchy, as outlined in Chapter 4. The book contains a useful book-list for formal analysis.

Index